GEORGINA O'SULLIVAN
COOKING AT THE BALLYMORE INN

GEORGINA O'SULLIVAN

First published in 2015 by Estragon Press for The Ballymore Inn, Ballymore Eustace, County Kildare, Ireland

© The Ballymore Inn

Text and Recipes and Food Styling © Georgina O'Sullivan

ISBN 978-1-906927-22-6

Text, Recipes and Food Styling by Georgina O'Sullivan
Photographs on pages 58, 80, 144, 176, 191 by Joanne Murphy
All other Photographs by Barry O'Sullivan
Props with thanks to Newbridge Silverware

Editor: John McKenna
Art Direction: Sally McKenna
Copy Editor: Judith Casey

Printed in Spain by Graphycems

CONTENTS

4. FROM THE GARDEN 59

The Ballymore Inn Tomato and Bread Soup ✳ Rosemary Sauté Potatoes ✳ Grilled Flatbreads with Sliced Steak and Baba Ghanoush ✳ Chargrilled Irish Beef Burger with Melted Cheddar ✳ Fried West Cork Buffalo Halloumi with Tomato and Avocado Salsa ✳ Duncannon Hake with Green Chilli and Lime Dressing and Cucumber Salad ✳ Lemon Cake with Lemon Balm Syrup ✳ Blackcurrant Fool ✳ Rich Chocolate Pots with Honeycomb ✳ Pistachio Meringues with Lemon Curd and Summer Berries ✳ Orange and Almond Tuiles ✳ Lemon and Sugar Biscuits.

5. YOU'RE INVITED 81

Chicken Liver Paté with Pistachio Nuts and Plum Relish ✳ Pork Rillette ✳ Gougères ✳ Hummus with Warm Flatbread ✳ Irish Stew with Caper and Parsley Dressing ✳ Fiery Fish Stew ✳ Chinese Slow Roast Shoulder of Pork ✳ Penang Beef with Fresh Green Chutney ✳ Kashmiri Chicken Curry ✳ Coconut, Lime and Pecan Ice Cream ✳ Hot Chocolate and Salted Caramel Puddings ✳ Cranberry and Orange Cake.

6. HOTTEST BBQS 101

Barbecued Dry-Aged Fillet Steaks with Asparagus and Parsley Dressing ✳ Sichuan Lamb Kebabs with Char-grilled Limes with Carrot and Chilli Salad ✳ Poached and Barbecued Chicken ✳ Barbecued Seafood Salad ✳ Boulangere Potatoes ✳ Monkfish Kebabs on Lemongrass Skewers with Grilled Fennel and Chilli ✳ Char-grilled Summer Vegetables ✳ Green Beans with Hazelnuts and Black Olives ✳ Tabbouleh Salad.

7. SUNDAY ROASTS 119

Beef Pot Roast ✳ Honey Roast Rack of Bacon with Stir-fry Cabbage, Shallot and Mustard Sauce ✳ Indian Roast Leg of Lamb ✳ Italian Roast Stuffed Peppers with Braised Black Beans and Pesto ✳ Lemon, Thyme and Garlic Roast Chicken ✳ Roast Belly of Pork with Pak Choi and Pineapple Salsa ✳ Roast Monkfish with Potatoes and Salsa Verde ✳ Roast Rib of Beef with Fresh Horseradish ✳ Slow Roast Shoulder of Lamb with Middle Eastern Rice and Lentils ✳ Rolled Pork Belly with Apple and Apricot Stuffing.

FOREWORD BY JOHN McKENNA

"Once in a blue moon, someone makes a progression in Irish food which seems to me to be important. I think what Georgina and Barry O'Sullivan are doing in The Ballymore Inn is important." I wrote that in June of 1998, in a review of The Ballymore Inn which appeared in the Weekend section of *The Irish Times*, under the headline "All the right ingredients".

Not only was that a reckless thing to suggest, it was – thankfully – correct. Today, if I were to write about the cooking in The Ballymore Inn, I would say exactly the same thing: what Barry and Georgina are doing – after twenty years in business – remains important, both to the idea of Irish food, and to the reputation of Irish food.

The importance lies in the fact that Mrs O'Sullivan's cooking is not like anyone else's, yet it seems to know everything about everyone else's cooking, whilst remaining entirely her own. She is a relentless culinary autodidact, subsuming restaurant experiences and cookery books with glee, then turning the influences into her own culinary language. Every visit to The Ballymore Inn is not just a chance to eat her food: it is also a chance to see what she has learnt since your last visit.

When you cook the recipes from this book, you will see that her stresses, her accents, her grace notes and her blue notes, are different from anyone else's. What initially appears conventional becomes, in her hands, something entirely unconventional. Like the best cooks, she has many gifts – coolness, imagination, clarity, stamina, taste – but she also has a way of subverting orthodoxy to make something seem brand new.

This is a trait she shares with the greatest female cooks – with Myrtle Allen of Ballymaloe House, with Judy Rogers of Zuni Café, or April Bloomfield of The Spotted Pig – iconic figures whose culinary worldview has always been set just left-of-centre, chefs who think it through, work it out, and create something that fizzes with originality every time they send a dish out of the kitchen.

Like those great cooks, Mrs O'Sullivan has one objective: deliciousness. There is no grandstanding in her work, no self-consciousness. Instead, there is a steely focus on what works, what works together, what works best. In all of these dishes, with their often surprising congress of ingredients, that is the inevitable outcome: deliciousness. That reason explains why The Ballymore Inn is one of the most successful restaurants in Ireland today, and has been for the last two decades.

In transforming her restaurant dishes into the language of the domestic kitchen, Georgina O'Sullivan gives us the techniques and secrets that have made her a cult figure in Irish cooking.

INTRODUCTION BY GEORGINA O'SULLIVAN

I hope that the recipes in this book all demonstrate a simple truth about cooking, which is that food creates an emotional connection between those who cook, and those who eat what the cook has made.

When we cook and when we eat, we enjoy not just the delicious things from the garden, the farm and the seas, transformed by the secrets of the kitchen, but also the warmth and comfort of great food, the fun and society of great cooking, the humour and celebration of sharing beautiful things to eat.

For the last twenty years my cooking has taken place in The Ballymore Inn, working alongside my husband, Barry. Our plan was to serve nice food, and interesting wines, and we have been fortunate to gather a quixotic band of suppliers who think like us and work the way we do.

We have also found an appreciative audience, and for our audience we have tried to continue to learn and improve, to keep discovering new ways to express the language of cooking and food. And it has been with this audience in mind that I have organised and adapted this collection of recipes. I hope that people will use the book and say: "You know, let's give this a shot." Hopefully, by following the instructions, the result will turn out well, and the cook will get a great response from their audience, and be encouraged to try other new things.

It is strange that we live in a modern society where people feel the need to ask the question: "Why cook?" The answer, of course, is because it is worth it, worth the time, worth the little bit of trouble that good cooking involves. When we cook, we are engaged with the world, with our ingredients, with the final result of making people happy. There is therapy in cooking, and cooking is time well spent, for it is time that delivers delicious, life-affirming results.

Georgina O'Sullivan

Ballymore Inn,
September 2015

KITCHEN BASICS

The secret is: get the basics right and you're more than half way there. Good bread, handmade each morning. Dry-aged West Cork beef from select Irish farms. The delicious flavour of Slaney Lamb. Fresh fish from Duncannon. Our own garden produce, just picked. These are our essentials to great food but there are also the extras which are always available in the kitchen. Here are the top staples we just couldn't do without.

CHICKEN STOCK

Irreplaceable in The Ballymore Inn kitchen, the stock is made every other day and serves as a base for sauces, braises and soups. Homemade chicken stock will transform the dish and is not at all difficult to do: take the chicken carcass/bones/wing tips, cover with cold water, add some chopped onion, carrot, leek, a few sprigs of thyme, bay leaf and peppercorns, bring the lot to the boil, skimming off any foam that forms on the surface, reduce to simmer and cook for 2 hours. Strain and cool, store in the fridge for 3-4 days or freeze for 2-3 months. If you just have the carcass of a roast chicken or two it's still well worth making the stock.

HOUSE VINAIGRETTE

For salads, the oil and vinegar should be the same quality as the leaves. The proportions are two thirds oil and one third vinegar plus a teaspoon of Dijon mustard. You can mix the oils, one third olive to two thirds sunflower. Blend the mustard with the vinegar and season then add the oils in a steady stream, whisking constantly. Store covered in the fridge for up to a week.

PRESERVED LEMONS

This is a simple method for preserving lemons; a great seasoning for salads, dressings, stews and essential for couscous. Slice the lemons into paper thin slices, layer the slices in a storage box with a sprinkling of salt and sugar, cover and store in the fridge for 24 hours. Pour olive oil over the lemons to cover and return to the fridge for 3 days. They will keep for 3-4 weeks and you can use the oil for other uses.

SLOW-ROASTED TOMATOES

We use these for tomato aioli and also for pasta sauce, tomato vinaigrette, and goat's cheese salad. Set the oven to its lowest setting, halve the tomatoes and place in a single layer, cut side up, on a baking sheet, sprinkle with a dusting of sugar, salt and pepper. Roast for 4/5 hours until they shrivel up, remove and cool, store in the fridge covered with a layer of olive oil, use within a few days.

AIOLI

A lovely thick garlicky mayonnaise, great with grilled fish, poached chicken, potato salad or stirred into seafood stew at the last minute. It can also be flavoured with tarragon, slow-roasted tomatoes, rocket, sorrel, all of them delicious. To make it, crush 3-4 cloves of garlic to a paste with some sea salt in the food processor, combine the garlic with 2 free range egg yolks and the juice of half a lemon, slowly add 250ml mild olive oil or half olive oil and half sunflower oil. As the sauce begins to thicken, you can add the oil a little more quickly. Store in the fridge for 2-3 days.

GARLIC CONFIT

We use garlic confit in so many preparations we consider it a kitchen staple, it's such a great flavouring device, and the oil the garlic is cooked in can be used as well. Place peeled cloves of garlic in a small saucepan and add enough oil to cover. Place over a very low heat and cook gently for 40-45 minutes, until the cloves are completely tender when pierced with a tip of a knife. Remove from the heat and allow the garlic to cool in the oil, store in the fridge submerged in the oil for up to a month.

SWEET & SOUR RED ONIONS

Perfect with pâté, terrines, chicken salads and char-grilled steak sandwiches. To prepare, take 2-3 onions, peeled and thinly sliced, place in a bowl with 3 tablespoons light brown sugar and 3 tablespoons red wine vinegar. Mix well together and store covered in the fridge for a week.

OVEN-ROASTED PEPPERS

Oven roasted peppers have a delicious mellow flavour and moist flesh. They are great in salads and are especially good on goat's cheese pizza. Set the oven to 200°C/ Gas 6. Line a baking sheet with foil. Cut the peppers in half, remove the seeds and stem, toss in olive oil, lay skin side up on the baking sheet, sprinkle with sea salt, and bake for 30-40 minutes until skin blisters and blackens. Remove from the oven, put the peppers in a bowl and cover tightly with cling wrap. The heat will cause the skin to bubble and separate from the flesh. When they're cool enough to handle, the skin can be removed easily. Use immediately or store in the fridge covered in olive oil.

BASIL OIL

We use this to finish many dishes, and it will keep well for up to a week in the fridge. To make, take 2-3 bunches of basil, place the leaves in the processor with 2-3 cloves of garlic, salt and pepper, whiz together, then trickle in 250ml of mild olive oil or half olive oil and half sunflower oil. Taste and adjust the seasoning. Store in the fridge.

THE BALLYMORE INN FRIES

We take as much care with the fries as with any of the more expensive dishes. We use Maris Pipers for their high dry matter. Each week, 400kg of the potatoes are peeled and hand-cut, then soaked in cold water overnight to remove the excess starch. They are drained, then dried with kitchen towels. The first fry cooks the potatoes thoroughly, leaving the interior fluffy. The second fry crisps the exterior, the natural sugars caramelize in the high heat and this turns the fries crisp and brown at the edge. Simply finish with a sprinkling of sea salt... delicious.

TOMATO RELISH

Great with lots of dishes – barbecues, sausages for brunch, steak sandwiches – and it will keep well in the fridge for a few days. Take 1-2 tablespoons oil, 1 large onion, finely chopped, 2-3 cloves garlic, chopped, 1 teaspoon smoked paprika, 1 x 400g can chopped tomatoes, 6 cherry tomatoes, chopped, 1 red chilli, finely chopped, 1 tablespoon red wine vinegar, 1 teaspoon sugar; a sprig of thyme; a squeeze of lemon, a dash of Worcestershire sauce, salt and black pepper. To cook, heat a deep pan, add the oil and sauté the onions and garlic for 3-4 minutes until golden brown, add the smoked paprika and cook for another minute, then add the tomatoes, chilli, vinegar, sugar, thyme, lemon juice, Worcestershire sauce and seasoning. Simmer gently for 15 minutes, stirring occasionally until well reduced. Check the seasoning. Remove from the heat and cool to serve.

Chapter 1

quick FIXES

No time to cook? Too exhausted to think at the end of the day? Here's the good news: with just a small amount of planning, shopping and having a reasonable store cupboard, delicious meals won't seem like a chore. Very soon you will realise that there is no end to the possibilities, no matter how little time you might have! And remember: a fresh nutritious meal is not only good for your health, it soothes the soul.

ARDSALLAGH GOAT'S CHEESE BRUSCHETTA *with* TOASTED HAZELNUTS

This is one of our most popular goat's cheese dishes; at home it makes a perfect quick supper.

[SERVES 2 /15 MINUTES /EASY]

2 large slices of good bread
drizzle of olive oil
2 tablespoons redcurrant jelly
160g Ardsallagh soft goat's cheese
about 100g rocket leaves
salt and black pepper
50g hazelnuts, toasted and roughly chopped
seasoning
aged balsamic vinegar to finish

Drizzle each slice of bread with a little olive oil. Toast under a hot grill on one side, now spread the redcurrant jelly over the untoasted side, then spread each slice with the goat's cheese. Place back under the grill for a few minutes until nicely toasted.

Place the bruschetta on the serving plates, toss the rocket in olive oil and seasoning, add the hazelnuts and serve with the bruschetta, finishing each one with some good-quality balsamic.

To toast hazelnuts, heat a dry pan, and add the nuts. Cook until they become fragrant. Tip the nuts onto a clean tea towel, and rub them together to remove the skins. Then chop roughly.

POTATO *and* ONION OMELETTE

At the Inn, we stick to the Spanish version made only with potatoes and onions. At home, it makes the best supper served with tomato and green chilli salsa, and good bread. A Spanish au pair who stayed with us many years ago, who was from Galicia, taught us the correct way to make the omelette, and it was a revelation: the potatoes must be small, the onion must be finely sliced, and they must be cooked separately to ensure that both are just right. So: use two pans to begin, make sure that the eggs and the potato and onion mixture are well mixed, and be generous with the olive oil. Turning the omelette can be a little awkward, but this gives a much better result that placing the omelette under the grill. All these little details in the preparation come together to transform something simple into something sublime.

[SERVES 3-4 /20 MINUTES /EASY]

100ml (5 tablespoons) olive oil	**cherry tomato & green chilli salsa**
8 medium potatoes, peeled and diced	20 cherry tomatoes, chopped
salt & black pepper	2 green chillies, finely chopped
2 large onions, thinly sliced	2 tablespoons chopped fresh coriander
6 eggs	3-4 tablespoons olive oil
	salt & black pepper

Heat 3 tablespoons of the oil in a non-stick pan, add the potatoes and season well, cook over a medium heat till golden brown and crispy. In another pan, heat 1 tablespoon of oil and sauté the onions until golden.

In a large bowl beat the eggs and season. Add the onions to the eggs, then add the potatoes to the egg mixture and mix well.

Heat the remaining oil in the pan and pour the mixture back into the pan. Cook until lightly golden on the base. Place an inverted plate, slightly larger than the pan, on top of the pan and turn out the omelette on to it. Then slide it back into the pan, and cook the other side until the eggs are set. Turn on to a serving plate or board, serve warm cut into wedges.

Mix all the salsa ingredients together with the seasoning. Serve a spoonful with the omelette.

CRISPY PORK *with* PAK CHOI *and* NOODLES

This recipe needs high, high heat, but it's simple enough for a quick midweek dinner. Don't be afraid of the heat, and stay with this dish: it needs your attention.

2 loin Irish pork chops, fat removed and cut into thin slices

marinade

2 tablespoons soy sauce

2 tablespoons sesame oil

$^1/_2$ tablespoon cornflour

dipping sauce

3 tablespoons rice vinegar

$^1/_2$ tablespoon sugar

1 tablespoon soy sauce

1 small red chilli, chopped finely

1-2 tablespoons sunflower oil

100g Chinese noodles, soaked in boiling water for 4 minutes, drained

50g pak choi, finely chopped

extra red chilli, chopped (optional)

Place the sliced pork in a bowl, add the marinade ingredients and mix well.

Next prepare the dipping sauce – heat the rice vinegar and sugar together in a small saucepan over a gentle heat until the sugar is dissolved, add the soy sauce and chilli, pour into a small bowl to serve.

Heat a wok or pan over a high heat, add a tablespoon of oil and stir fry the pork in two batches until crispy and fully cooked. Add the noodles, pak choi and chilli and a little more oil, if necessary. Stir fry the lot until the noodles are heated through. Serve with the dipping sauce on the side.

Make extra dipping sauce, as it keeps really well, and is very good with chicken or char-grilled vegetables.

SPICY LAMB FLATBREADS *with* YOGURT *and* POMEGRANATE

A 'dig in and help yourself' supper for two or more – just double up the recipe as required. I find that I long for bread that speaks to me with its goodness, so good bread here is critical, and the bread lends to sharing the dish.

[SERVES 2 /30 MINUTES /EASY]

2 tablespoons sunflower oil	2-4 flatbreads, buy or make ahead and
2 red onions, thinly sliced	freeze (page 54) or use pitta bread
350g minced Irish lamb	salad leaves, a few handfuls
2-3 cloves garlic, crushed	6-8 cherry tomatoes, chopped
1 teaspoon sumac	1 lime, cut into wedges
1 red chilli, chopped	olive oil
1 tablespoon pomegranate	a few mint leaves, chopped
molasses	2-3 tablespoons Greek-style yogurt
salt & black pepper	1 pomegranate, seeded

Heat half the oil in a wide shallow pan. Sauté the onion until it caramelises. Remove from the pan, then heat the remaining oil and sauté the lamb in batches so that it colours well. When all the lamb is cooked and crispy at the edges, add the cooked onion, stir in the garlic, sumac, chilli, and molasses, then season.

Warm the flatbreads or pitta, arrange them on a serving plate or dish with the lamb, the salad leaves, cherry tomatoes and lime wedges. Season the salad with salt, black pepper, a drizzle of olive oil and a squeeze of lime. Scatter the mint over the lamb, and serve with a bowl of yogurt and pomegranate seeds on the side. Invite everybody to help themselves: just roll up and eat!

This also works well for a party; keep the lamb and bread warm and allow guests to assemble and choose their own toppings.

BLACKENED COD *with* YOGURT *and* SPICE

This beautiful yogurt and spice mix takes influences from the cooking of the west coast of India. If you need to take a shortcut and use a shop spice mix, that's fine, but it's fun to get into gathering and toasting the spices for the dish.

4 x 180g fillets of sustainable cod,
  hake or haddock
1-2 tablespoons olive oil for frying

yogurt & spice mix
¹/₂ teaspoon cumin seeds
¹/₂ teaspoon coriander seeds
pinch of chilli flakes
¹/₂ teaspoon turmeric
4-5 tablespoons Greek-style yogurt
1 tablespoon fresh ginger, chopped
2 cloves garlic, chopped
2 tablespoon fresh coriander, chopped
salt & black pepper
1 lime, cut into wedges to serve

Place the fillets of fish on a flat shallow tray, keep refrigerated until ready to cook. Prepare the spice mix - toast the cumin and coriander seeds in a small, dry pan for a minute until fragrant. Remove from the heat and grind in a spice/coffee grinder or pestle and mortar.

Tip the spices into a bowl, add the chilli, turmeric, yogurt, ginger, garlic, fresh coriander and seasoning. Mix together well, spread a little of the mixture over each fillet - keep the remainder to serve with the fish.

To cook, heat a large heavy pan, add the oil and cook the fish for 3-4 minutes on each side. Serve with a bowl of basmati rice, stir-fried greens, the remaining spice mixture on the side, and wedges of lime.

SPAGHETTI *with* FRIED BROCCOLI, KALE *and* HAZELNUT PESTO

Make sure to get the mingle here: keep turning and turning your ingredients in the pan! Make extra pesto for another day; it's good with grilled chicken or fish.

[SERVES 4 /30 MINUTES /EASY]

hazelnut pesto
100g hazelnuts, toasted and roughly
  chopped
2-3 tablespoons olive oil
grated rind & juice of half a lemon
40g Parmesan, grated
handful of flat-leaf parsley, chopped
salt & black pepper

400g broccoli, cut into florets
handful of kale, chopped finely
2-3 anchovy fillets, chopped
400g spaghetti, cooked (keep warm with a little of the cooking water)

To make the pesto, place half the hazelnuts in the processor with 2 tablespoons of the oil. Add the lemon rind and juice, Parmesan and parsley, then whiz together, check seasoning and set aside.

Next heat the remaining oil in a large pan. Cook the broccoli in the hot oil until nicely charred, stir in the kale and anchovy fillets. Mix well, tip the warm spaghetti into the pan, then stir the pesto through the pasta. Divide between warm serving bowls and garnish with the remaining hazelnuts, extra Parmesan and a drizzle of olive oil.

If you need a vegetarian option, just drop the anchovies.

CHARGRILLED PORK *with* PASTA IN CAPER SAUCE

A lovely simple supper, but be careful where you buy your pork chops: they can be tough because some outlets sell them too fresh, so get them from a good craft butcher who ages the meat. I like to marinate the pork overnight, or longer if possible.

[SERVES 4 /30 MINUTES /EASY]

4 Irish pork chops, cut from the rack, bone in, not
  too lean - for flavour
marinade
juice and rind of a lemon
Few sage leaves
2 tablespoons olive oil
salt and black pepper

white wine and caper sauce
1 tablespoon olive oil
knob of butter
1 tablespoon capers, drained
2-3 garlic cloves, chopped
glass of white wine
250ml stock or reserved pasta water
1 tablespoon Dijon mustard
1 tablespoon crème fraiche
300g – 400g tagliatelle, cooked and kept warm

Place the chops in a deep dish with the lemon juice and rind, sage leaves, olive oil and seasoning, leave to marinate for a few hours or overnight.

To make the sauce, heat the olive oil and butter in a deep pan, add capers and sauté for a minute, stir in the garlic and wine, bring to the boil and reduce by half. Add the stock or pasta water, stir in the mustard and crème fraiche and simmer until the sauce begins to thicken, taste for seasoning. Meanwhile cook the chops on a heavy cast-iron grill pan for about 5-6 minutes on each side.

To serve, place the pasta on deep plates, arrange cutlet on top and pour the sauce over the pork. A bowl of lightly cooked spinach would be perfect as a side dish.

COCONUT CHICKEN *with* CORIANDER SALSA

Assemble the ingredients and cook in the oven – giving you time to take a walk or clear the emails! This dish is very good served with a bowl of boiled rice. And here's a handy tip: to make your lime juicier, pop it into the microwave for 5 seconds.

[SERVES 4 /20 MINUTES, PLUS 45-50 MINUTES COOKING /EASY]

2kg free-range Irish chicken, jointed into
  8 pieces on the bone
salt & black pepper
2 tablespoon sunflower oil
2-3 cloves garlic, chopped
2-3 lemongrass stems, chopped
400ml can coconut milk
few handfuls of baby spinach

coriander salsa
2-3 shallots, finely chopped
2 red chillies, finely chopped
2 tablespoon fresh coriander,
  chopped
juice & rind of 1 lime
1 tablespoon honey
1 tablespoon sunflower oil
salt & black pepper

Set oven to Gas 4 /180°C. Season the chicken, heat the oil in a large flameproof pan and sauté the chicken in the pan until nicely browned. Add the garlic, lemongrass and coconut milk. Bring to the boil, cover the pan and place in the preheated oven for about 45-50 minutes or until the chicken is fully cooked.

Use a meat thermometer to check the temperature is 75°C. Stir in the spinach and check seasoning. Mix all the salsa ingredients together. Just before serving, spoon the salsa over the chicken.

TURBOT *with* FRIED GARLIC, SMOKED PAPRIKA *and* CHERRY TOMATO DRESSING

Lovely Spanish flavours here for a special night in, but if it's just a regular Wednesday, hake or cod will do very well in place of the pricier turbot!

[SERVES 4 /30 MINUTES /EASY]

4 x 180g fillets of turbot
salt & black pepper,
olive oil for frying
knob of butter

cherry tomato dressing
3 tablespoons olive oil
4-6 cloves garlic, cut into thin
  slivers
1 teaspoon smoked paprika
1 red chilli, finely chopped
dash of sherry or red wine vinegar
12-16 cherry tomatoes, chopped
2 tablespoons fresh coriander,
  chopped
salt & pepper

Place the fish in a flat dish, season with salt, pepper and olive oil, keep in the fridge until you are ready to cook.

Make up the dressing – heat the 3 tablespoons olive oil in a pan, add the garlic and just allow to turn golden brown. Stir in the paprika and chilli, cook for a minute, then stir in the sherry or red wine vinegar. Remove from the heat, stir in the tomatoes and coriander, and season. Set aside and keep just warm.

To cook the fish, heat a large non-stick pan and add about a tablespoon of oil. When it's really hot, place the fish in the pan, skin side up, cook for 3-4 minutes until it's just turning golden at the edges. Add the knob of butter just before you turn the fish, and you'll have beautiful golden brown fillets, cook for another 2 minutes and you are done. Serve with the dressing and a dish of lightly cooked spinach on the side – perfect!

STEAK SANDWICH *with* MELTED GUBBEEN *and* CARAMELISED RED ONION

This is the best home alone supper you can imagine! You can use a variety of cheeses – Taleggio is also really good – but Gubbeen farmhouse cheese, from the Ferguson family of West Cork, is sublime.

[SERVES 1 /20 MINUTES /EASY]

1 x 150g dry-aged Irish sirloin steak
Salt & black pepper
balsamic vinegar
2 tablespoons olive oil
1 x 50g slice Gubbeen cheese
2 slices of good bread
handful of salad leaves

caramelised red onion
1 tablespoon olive oil
knob of butter
2 red onions, thinly sliced
1 teaspoon pomegranate molasses
salt & black pepper

To make the caramelised onions, heat a heavy pan with the olive oil and a knob of butter. Sauté the onions gently until they caramelise - about 10 minutes - stir in the molasses and season well. Set aside.

Place the steak on a dish and season well with salt, pepper, balsamic vinegar and oil. Heat a cast-iron ridged pan until hot, cook the steak for 2-3 minutes on each side for medium. Drizzle the bread with a little olive oil and toast on the pan at the same time.

Two minutes before the end of cooking time, cover the steak with the cheese. Cover the pan for a minute, to allow the cheese to melt, and toss the salad leaves with a drizzle of olive oil. Serve on the bread with the steak, the caramelised onions and some Ballymore Inn Tomato Chutney on the side.

CHARGRILLED CHICKEN *and* CASHEW NUT SALAD *with* MANGO DRESSING

You can make this for a quick supper, or for a large gathering as it's a great crowd pleaser! The secret of the dish lies with the texture given by the toasted cashew nuts, and with the ripeness of the mango: ripeness is all! When you are buying the mango, give it a gentle squeeze to see if it's ready, and then look after it carefully until you use it.

[SERVES 4 /30 MINUTES /EASY]

4 free-range Irish chicken breasts, skin on	**mango dressing**
salt & black pepper	1 mango, sliced
200g cashew nuts, toasted	3-4 scallions, chopped
1 mango, sliced	1 red chilli, chopped
4 handfuls mixed leaves	1 tablespoon rice vinegar
juice of 1 lime	1 tablespoon sweet chilli sauce
1 tablespoon olive oil	1 tablespoon olive oil
salt & black pepper	salt & black pepper

Season the chicken well and cook on a cast-iron ridged pan, until fully cooked. Keep warm.

Make the dressing – place all the ingredients in the processor and blend together, check the seasoning, pour the dressing into a bowl and set aside.

Mix the cashew nuts, mango, salad leaves, lime juice, olive oil and seasoning together in a large bowl, divide between four plates. Slice the chicken and arrange on top of the salad with a spoonful of the dressing. Any leftover dressing will keep for 3-4 days. It's also a good topping for grilled pork.

Chapter 2

best BRUNCH

The idea of a lazy late breakfast or brunch has great appeal, enjoying good bread, fresh juices and something substantial like French toast with bacon, or grilled sausages with Lyonnaise potatoes, because everybody is always starving at this hour. It might also involve taking in a long walk or a cycle, then back for brunch with family and friends, and there is no better way for an informal get together. So, make a plan – bread made; juice ready; poached fruits; good granola. Table set, then get everybody out in the fresh air. When you arrive back, allow the guests to help themselves to fruit and granola, this gives you time to cook the sausages or poach the eggs, make the coffee, and serve up... with lots of chat and more coffee.

SPINACH OMELETTE *with* COOLEA CHEESE *and* GRILLED CHERRY TOMATOES

This is a really delicious brunch favourite but it can also be the best home alone dinner when you are too tired to even chop an onion. Get a non-stick 25cm pan and keep it just for omelettes. The Coolea brings a sweet fudgyness to the dish.

[SERVES 1 /15 MINUTES /EASY]

3 eggs
3 teaspoons water
salt & black pepper
2 handfuls baby spinach, finely chopped
6-8 cherry tomatoes, seasoned & brushed with olive oil
knob of butter
60g Coolea cheese, grated

Beat the eggs, water, seasoning and spinach together in a medium-sized bowl. Heat the grill and cook the tomatoes for 4-5 minutes until just soft. Keep warm. Heat a non-stick omelette pan and add the knob of butter. Pour in the egg mixture and allow it to cook for about a minute, then draw in the edges, tilting the pan so the un-cooked liquid runs on to the base of the pan. Continue until the omelette is cooked to your taste, fold over one third, starting at the handle end, add the grated cheese along the centre, slide the omelette down the pan and tip it onto the serving plate. Serve with the grilled tomatoes and good bread.

best BLT

A properly ripe avocado; the best bacon you can afford; crisp cos lettuce for crunch; satisfyingly chewy sourdough bread; and sweet basil mayo. Every detail counts when it comes to making the best BLT, so pay a little extra to have the finest ingredients to hand, and then everything combines magically to make this the most special sandwich.

[MAKES 2 /20 MINUTES /EASY]

1 beef tomato
salt
4 thick slices of Irish streaky bacon
4 slices sourdough bread
olive oil
4-6 cos leaves
1 avocado, peeled & sliced
basil mayonnaise (see watercress aioli page 36, and replace the watercress with basil)

Starting with the tomato, slice thinly with a serrated knife, sprinkle with salt and leave on a sheet of kitchen towel for 10 minutes to rid it of excess liquid – no soggy sandwich here! Next grill the bacon on a cast-iron grill pan until cooked. Drizzle the bread with olive oil. When the bacon is cooked, remove from the pan and keep warm. Clean the pan if necessary and grill the bread on the same pan, on each side. Place the toasted bread on the serving plate or board, cover with the lettuce then add the sliced tomato, bacon and avocado. Top with the basil mayonnaise and cover with the second slice of grilled bread. Eat immediately.

BLACK PUDDING *with* APPLE, BACON *and* BALSAMIC

Irish black pudding is the perfect deal when you want something quick, simple and satisfying. The balsamic adds viscosity, and nicely counterpoints the apples.

[SERVES 4 /20 MINUTES /EASY]

---

1 tablespoon sunflower oil
200g black pudding, broken into pieces
100g Irish streaky bacon, diced
4 handfuls mixed leaves
1 tablespoon olive oil
juice of half lemon
salt & black pepper
2 crisp eating apples, core removed, not peeled, thinly sliced
aged balsamic vinegar

To cook, heat a large pan, add the oil and sauté the black pudding for 3-4 minutes, remove from the pan and keep warm. Add the bacon and cook till crispy, set aside. Toss the salad leaves with the olive oil, lemon juice and seasoning, then divide between four serving plates. Arrange the apple slices on each plate. Return the black pudding to the bacon in the pan, reheat for a minute or two, then spoon over the salad and drizzle with balsamic vinegar. Serve immediately.

BLUEBERRY FRIANDS

I was given this recipe by the chef at the Crittenden Estate Winery in the Mornington Peninsula in Australia, which has both great wines and great baking. Just out of the oven they make a great addition to any brunch table.

[MAKES 12 /20 MINUTES /EASY]

185g butter, melted
6 egg whites
225g icing sugar
75g plain flour
125g ground almonds
zest of 1 lemon
60g blueberries

Set oven to Gas 4/180˚C. Brush each mould with a little of the melted butter. Whisk the egg whites to just soft peaks, sift the icing sugar and whisk into the egg whites. Fold in the flour, ground almonds, lemon zest and blueberries, followed by the remaining melted butter. Divide the mixture between the moulds, bake for 25-30 minutes until nicely browned. Serve warm.

You will need 12 friand moulds, which are slightly oval shaped, or just use muffin cases.

CRAB CAKES with WATERCRESS and LIME AIOLI

The secret here, of course, is the quality of the crab meat you use – fresh only, in pieces or lumps, not shredded – and the next most important point is to use more crab and less cake: after that it's simple. Handling the ingredients lightly is important, as you don't want to overwork the mixture.

[MAKES 8 /20 MINUTES /EASY]

80g breadcrumbs
1 teaspoon mustard powder
salt & black pepper
pinch cayenne
pinch paprika
3 tablespoons flat-leaf parsley,
   finely chopped
450g fresh crab (white meat only)
2 eggs, beaten
seasoned flour to coat
1 tablespoon sunflower oil,
knob of butter
1 lime cut into wedges to serve
bunch of watercress

To make the crab cakes, in a large bowl, mix the breadcrumbs, mustard, seasoning, cayenne, paprika and parsley together, gently mix in the crab, and add the beaten eggs a little at a time. Shape into eight cakes, flatten slightly, and coat each one in the seasoned flour. Refrigerate until ready to cook.

To cook the crab cakes, heat a large non-stick pan with a tablespoon of sunflower oil and a knob of butter. Cook the crab cakes for 3-4 minutes on each side. Serve immediately with the aioli, extra watercress and lime wedges.

See recipe overleaf for Watercress & Lime Aioli.

WATERCRESS and LIME AIOLI

2 egg yolks
salt
scant teaspoon Dijon mustard
225ml sunflower oil, or half
  sunflower oil and half olive oil
2 tablespoons watercress, finely
chopped
squeeze of lime juice

To make the aioli, put the egg yolks in the processor with a little salt and the mustard. Very slowly – drop by drop - add the oil with the motor running. As the mixture begins to thicken you can

If the worst happens and the aioli separates – all is not lost, start again with another egg yolk and add back the separated mixture, this time slowly, slowly until it all comes together.

add the remaining oil a little faster. Add the watercress and lime juice to taste. Keep the aioli in the fridge till serving. If you wish, you can add a spoonful of garlic confit (page 11) when you add the mustard.

FRENCH TOAST with CRISPY BACON and MAPLE SYRUP

Impossible to resist, but make sure you allow the bread to soak for at least 15 minutes before cooking. Also remember that the better the bread, the better the toast!

[SERVES 4 /30 MINUTES /EASY]

4 eggs
125 ml milk
8 slices bread (brioche if possible)
butter for cooking,
12 slices streaky bacon, grilled, keep warm
maple syrup

Mix the eggs and milk together. Pour the mixture into a shallow dish and soak the bread in the mixture for 15 minutes, turning from time to time. Heat a large non-stick pan, add a little butter and cook the French toast until golden on both sides. Serve with the grilled bacon and maple syrup.

FRUIT and HONEY GRANOLA

This will store well for 3-4 weeks. Each morning, stir a couple of spoonfuls through some Greek yogurt and drizzle with extra honey or maple syrup.

You can serve the granola with strawberries or raspberries during the summer months, and in winter with grated apple, pear or banana.

[25 PORTIONS /30 MINUTES PLUS 45 MINUTES BAKING /EASY]

1kg oat flakes
150g desiccated coconut
150g brown sugar
1 tablespoon sesame seeds
100g sunflower seeds
100g pumpkin seeds
150g peanuts
75g pistachio nuts
200g dried apricots, finely chopped
100g dried figs, finely chopped
250ml sunflower oil
300g honey

Set the oven to Gas 4/180˚C. Mix the oats, coconut, brown sugar, sesame seeds, sunflower seeds, pumpkin seeds, peanuts and pistachios in a large mixing bowl.

Put the apricots, figs, oil and honey into a saucepan, place over a gentle heat until the honey is dissolved. Remove from the heat, strain off the honey and oil and set the fruit aside. Pour the honey and oil into the mixing bowl with the oats, stir well through the oat mixture, tip the lot into a deep roasting tin and bake in the preset oven for 40-45 minutes. Stir the mixture every 15 minutes, making sure the edges don't burn. Stir in the apricots and figs for the final 15 minutes. Cool and store in an airtight container for 3-4 weeks.

GRILLED SAUSAGES *with* LYONNAISE POTATOES *and* RED ONION

Find the best quality sausages you can for this dish, which makes a very good addition to brunch. Artisanal and speciality sausages are now widely available throughout the country, and many of the best producers of good pork also make exceptional sausages, which lift the dish into another realm of deliciousness.

[SERVES 4 /30 MINUTES /EASY]

4 large sausages
2 tablespoons olive oil
8 medium potatoes,
   peeled & thickly sliced
2-3 red onions, sliced
2-3 garlic cloves, chopped
a generous knob of butter
salt & black pepper
handful of parsley, chopped

Heat a cast-iron grill pan and cook the sausages over a moderate heat until fully cooked, keep warm. While the sausages are cooking, heat the oil in another large shallow pan, sauté the potatoes until just turning golden brown, add the onions and continue to cook for another 4-5 minutes. When the potatoes and onions are just cooked, stir in the garlic, butter and season well. Add the parsley just before serving with some tomato relish (see page 12).

POACHED EGGS *with* PANCETTA *on* TOASTED CRUMPETS

Keep this dish for a special brunch for two people. This quantity of batter will make 12-14 crumpets; you can freeze what you don't use and toast them straight from the freezer. To make perfect poached eggs, drop the whole egg into the simmering water for a few seconds, lift them out then crack them back into the simmering water.

[SERVES 2 /50 MINUTES PREP PLUS 1 HOUR FOR THE BATTER TO REST /MODERATE]

crumpets (to make 12-14 crumpets)
450g strong flour
10g salt
15g fresh yeast
500ml water, warm

knob of butter
4 slices pancetta or Irish streaky bacon
100g mushrooms, chopped
4 eggs
chopped chives to garnish

griddle or cast-iron frying pan, 4 x 8cm crumpet rings

To make the crumpets, place the flour in a mixer bowl, add the salt and mix well. Blend the yeast with the warm water and set aside for 10 minutes. Then pour the yeast liquid into the flour and beat well to make a very thick, but smooth, batter. Cover and set aside for about an hour.

As the batter should not be too stiff (or your crumpets will not have holes) it's best to test one before cooking a whole batch. Heat the griddle or pan to very hot. Put a buttered crumpet ring on the griddle and pour about 2 soup spoons of the batter into the ring. If the holes don't form, add a little more water to the batter. Or if the batter is too thin and runs out under the ring, add a little extra flour to the mix. As soon as the upper surface is set and covered with holes, about 6-7 minutes, use a tea towel to ease off the ring. Flip the crumpet over with a palette knife to cook the other side for 2-3 minutes. Continue to cook the remaining batter, making the crumpets in batches. Keep warm in a folded tea towel.

Next sauté the pancetta and mushrooms together in a pan with the knob of butter, keep warm. In a large pan of simmering water, poach the eggs until just cooked to your taste. To serve, split the crumpets and toast on the hot griddle. Top with the pancetta and mushrooms then add the poached eggs. Garnish with the chopped chives to serve.

POACHED FRUITS *with* VANILLA *and* LEMON

The secret to perfectly poached fruit is to cook each fruit for just the right amount of time - don't add all the fruit to the cooking syrup together. So, for example, pears will take 10 minutes, and plums take 5 minutes, so start with the pears and after 5 minutes add the plums. Add the blueberries just before serving.

[SERVES 6 /30 MINUTES /EASY]

cooking syrup	fruit
1 glass white wine	6 small pears, peeled, cored & quartered
250g golden caster sugar	4-5 plums, stoned & quartered
750ml water	3-4 sticks rhubarb (optional) in season, chopped
zest & juice of 1 lemon	
1 vanilla pod, sliced lengthways	200g blueberries
pinch of saffron	Greek yogurt, to serve

In a large shallow pan, add the wine and reduce by half over a high heat. Add the sugar and water, allow the sugar to dissolve, then bring to the boil. Add the lemon juice and zest. Scrape the vanilla pod then add the seeds and pod to the pan with the saffron. Simmer for a few minutes then add the fruit, according to the cooking time. If using rhubarb, it will take 3 minutes. Scoop out the fruit from the syrup as it cooks and place on a serving dish.

Increase the heat and simmer the liquor for a further 5 minutes to reduce it to a syrup. Cool and pour it over the poached fruit. Add the blueberries just before serving, and pass around a bowl of Greek yogurt.

Chapter 3

UNBEATABLE

Bread

I love good bread...mixing, baking, the aroma and, best of all, the delicious eating! From our very first days, we've made our own bread, and it has always been one of our most important building blocks for good food and an essential part of our kitchen activities.

The day starts with the proving and baking of sourdough granary and baguettes, then the starter and leaven is mixed for the next day's batch. This is the corner stone of the bakery but we also make traditional soda bread on a Sunday morning, sesame baps for homemade burgers, naan bread for curries, brioche for pâté, flatbreads for hummus; we just can't imagine life without great bread. Here are some of our favourite recipes. In the Inn we use Odlums strong flour, stone ground wholemeal will give you extra flavour, as will sea salt. We use fresh yeast but you'll get good results with instant dried yeast – just use half the weight. Some breads need a bit of time and planning but none are complicated, and all are worth trying. You won't be disappointed.

TREACLE BREAD

In two hours, from start to finish, you will not only have the healthiest bread but also the most delicious. It's a great start to the day, but it's also good last thing at night, with a slice of goat's cheese and a good drizzle of honey.

[MAKES 1 X 1KG LOAF]

2 tablespoons oil
250g coarse wholemeal flour
250g strong white flour
1 teaspoon salt
1 sachet (7g) instant dried yeast
400ml warm water
1 tablespoon treacle

Brush a 1kg non-stick loaf tin with a little of the oil. Weigh out the flours in a large mixing bowl, add the salt and yeast, mix well. In a jug, mix the warm water with the treacle and the remaining oil. Pour the water and treacle mix into the flour mixture and mix well until it all comes together. Spoon into the tin, cover with a tea towel and leave in a warm spot, at about 20°C; it will be well risen in an hour.

Set the oven Gas 6/200°C. When the oven is hot, bake the loaf for about 1 hour – after 45 minutes remove from the tin and continue baking until the loaf sounds hollow when tapped on the base or use a probe - 98°C is just about right.

If you are new to bread making, start with this one - you'll be well pleased with the results.

Homemade Breads
Small Baguette €2.50
Large loaf €4.00

basic White Bread

Once you have mastered the recipe for treacle bread, and your baking confidence is on the rise, then have a go at this extraordinarily versatile white bread. We use this to make baguettes, we use it for our pizza bases, for our white loaves, to make our burger baps and also for our naan bread.

[MAKES 2 LOAVES OR 3 BAGUETTES]

700g white strong flour
15g sea salt
15g fresh yeast
1 teaspoon sugar
400ml warm water, plus more as needed

Place the flour and salt in a mixer bowl and mix together. Blend the yeast, sugar and a tablespoon of the water together, set aside for 10-15 minutes, then add to the flour and salt mixture with the remaining water. Knead with the dough hook for about 5 minutes until really smooth; it should not be too stiff, add a little more water as necessary.

Allow the dough to rise for about an hour then knead again for 2-3 minutes. The bread will have more flavour if it rises slowly. You can shape it into two loaves at this stage, place in two well-oiled loaf tins (450g) then leave to rest for 30 minutes. The dough is ready for baking when a small dent remains after the dough is pressed lightly with the finger.

Set the oven to Gas 7/220°C, brush the loaves with water and sprinkle with a pinch of sea salt. Bake for 30-40 minutes, reducing the heat to Gas 6/200°C after 20 minutes. The bread should sound hollow when it's fully cooked or use a digital probe, 98°C is just right, then cool on a wire rack. If it's more convenient, you can store the dough covered in an oiled bowl in the fridge overnight. This will also improve the flavour.

If it's more convenient, you can store the dough covered in an oiled bowl in the fridge overnight. This will also improve the flavour.

BAGUETTES

[MAKES 3 BAGUETTES]

1 x basic white bread recipe (previous page), taken to the first rising stage

Knock back the risen dough with your hands, then divide into three equal-sized pieces. Roll each piece into a sausage shape about 30cm long and 7cm thick (make sure you have a baking sheets this size), pleat a floured tea towel to make three moulds between the pleats to hold the pieces of dough while they are rising so they keep the traditional baguette shape. Cover with a damp tea towel and leave to rise until doubled in size, about an hour.

Meanwhile preheat the oven to Gas 7/220°C. Place a container of water in the oven to create steam during the baking. Remove the damp tea towel and roll the loaves on to the baking sheets. Using a sharp knife or razor blade, slash the top of each loaf several times, then brush with water and sprinkle with sea salt. Bake the baguettes for 20 minutes then reduce the temperature to Gas 6/200°C and bake for another 5-10 minutes. Cool on a wire rack.

NAAN BREAD

Delicious with Indian dishes, or for dipping into a tasty hummus. (See photo on previous page)

[MAKES ABOUT 25 NAAN]

1 x basic white bread recipe (see previous page)
melted butter
onion seeds

Set oven to Gas 7/220°C. Make the dough in the normal way and knock back. Take 60g pieces of dough and roll each piece into very thin round. Place rounds on a floured baking sheet, leave to rest for 20 minutes, then brush with some melted butter and sprinkle with onion seeds. Bake for 15-20 minutes.

You can replace some of the liquid in the basic recipe with Greek-style yogurt for extra flavour.

BURGER BAPS

We use these for homemade burgers, but they are very useful for any sandwich filling. Having a delicious, toothsome, satisfying bap is the real secret of enjoying the best home-made burger.

[MAKES ABOUT 12]

1 x basic white bread recipe (see page 47)
egg yolk mixed with sea salt
sesame seeds

Set oven to Gas 6/200°C. Make the dough in the normal way, knock back, knead for a few seconds and divide into about 12 x 120g pieces. Roll each one out to approximately 11 x 7cm, place well apart on floured baking sheets. Leave to rise for 20 minutes. Brush lightly with egg wash and sprinkle with sesame seeds. Press your thumb into the centre of each bap to make the surface flattish, rather than domed. Bake in the hot oven for 15 minutes.

BRIOCHE

This rich buttery bread has lots of uses in the kitchen, not to mention making the best ever French toast! Many of the recipes are quite involved but this one, which was given to me on a cookery course in France, works very well and is simple enough to make. It can be made the night before and baked in the morning for a lovely breakfast treat. The French chefs will argue about the amount of butter: we use half butter to flour, which is quite enough I think! Bake in the special brioche tins for the traditional fluted effect, or you can also use a loaf tin.

500g strong flour
1 teaspoon salt
1 tablespoon sugar
25g fresh yeast
70ml warm water
4 eggs, beaten
250g butter, room temperature
1 egg yolk, beaten with a little salt to glaze

Place the flour, salt and sugar in the mixer bowl. Blend the yeast with a table-spoon of the water and leave for 2-3 minutes. Add the blended yeast, the water, and the beaten eggs to the flour, mix until smooth and leave for about an hour. Next add the butter and mix again until well blended, smooth and glossy. Place in an oiled bowl and leave covered in cling wrap at room temperature for an hour or until double in size. Turn the dough on to a floured surface, knead lightly, return to the bowl, cover and leave in the fridge overnight.

Next day, knead the dough on a lightly floured surface. If you are using a brioche mould, divide the dough into one third for the top and remainder for the base. Butter the mould well, place the larger piece on the base, make a hole in the centre with your fingertips, roll the smaller piece into an elongated shape and gently press the narrow end into the centre of the large ball. Lightly brush the top with the egg yolk to glaze. Leave the dough to rise until almost double in size for about an hour. Prepare individual moulds in the same way.

Set the oven to Gas 6/200°C. Glaze the tops again and bake for 40-45 minutes, or 20-25 minutes for individual brioches. Serve warm with homemade raspberry jam for breakfast or toasted with pâté.

Serve warm with homemade raspberry jam for breakfast or toasted with pâté.

BROWN SODA BREAD

This is our Sunday morning bread - simple, fast to make, with no kneading necessary. Just place it in well-oiled tins, and you'll be eating it an hour later.

[MAKES TWO 1KG LOAVES]

500g wholewheat flour

500g plain white flour

1 tablespoon wheatgerm

2 teaspoons salt

2 teaspoons bread soda, sifted

800ml buttermilk

1 egg

2 teaspoons treacle

Set oven to Gas 6/200˚C. Oil two 1kg baking tins. Place all the dry ingredients in a large mixing bowl and mix well together. In a large jug whisk together the buttermilk, egg and treacle, pour into the flour mixture, stir well until everything is well mixed. Divide between the two oiled tins, place in the hot oven and bake for 40-50 minutes. Turn out of the tins and bake for a further 5-10 minutes; the loaves should sound hollow when tapped on the base. Wrap them in a tea towel to cool for a softer crust.

CIABATTA

The 'slipper' bread, as this is its
shape, has a delicious flavour,
open texture and chewy crust.
Dipped in olive oil, you'll agree it's
worth the effort. Start 24 hours
ahead as the starter dough needs
a long, slow rise. You will need an
electric mixer to achieve the right
texture and you'll also get better
results with fresh yeast: after that
it's very straightforward.

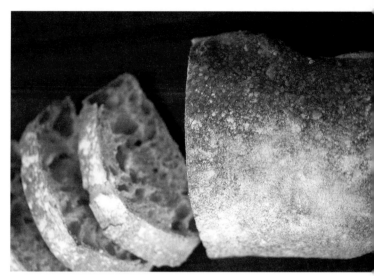

[MAKES 4 LOAVES]

starter dough	ciabatta	550ml starter mix
7g fresh yeast	7g fresh yeast	450g strong flour
350ml warm water	450ml warm water	20g salt
450g strong flour	1 tablespoon olive oil	

To make the starter, blend the yeast with a tablespoon of the warm water and
set aside for a few minutes. Mix the remaining water with the flour and add in the
blended yeast, mix again, remove to a lightly oiled bowl and leave to rise at a cool
room temperature for 24 hours.

To make the ciabatta, blend the yeast with a tablespoon of the warm water. Leave
for 4-5 minutes, then to the mixer bowl add the remaining water, oil and 550g of
starter. Mix well until blended, then add in the flour and salt, mix at high speed with
the dough hook for 10-15 minutes until the dough is pulling away from the sides of
the bowl. Place the dough in an oiled bowl, cover with a damp tea towel and leave
for about an hour until doubled in size.

Cut the dough into four pieces, and keeping your hands damp, stretch each piece
into a rectangle with your fingers, 30cm x 7cm. Flour two baking sheets, place two
loaves on each sheet, dimple the loaves with your fingertips so they won't rise too
much. Cover again with damp tea towels and leave for another 2 hours. Preheat the
oven to Gas 7/220°C, place a container of water in the oven to provide some steam
during the baking, dust the loaves with flour and bake for 25 minutes. Cool on a
wire rack.

FLAT *breads*

These are unleavened discs, and are ideal for scooping up tasty spicy foods. You simply cook the flatbreads on a heavy frying pan, so no oven is needed. As no yeast is used, this flatbread recipe is the perfect starting point for the cook who has never made bread before.

Each time I make flatbreads I am reminded of a visit to Egypt that included a trip to the desert to meet the local tribe. We were treated to mint tea and bread made just like this recipe but there was no cooker, just a fire on the sand and over the fire a very battered-looking upturned wok or karahi. When it was really hot they slapped on thin pieces of dough which they had stretched with their hands, then turned them over and cooked them on the other side.

[MAKES 8]

250g strong flour
1 teaspoon salt
150ml water
melted butter for
  brushing

Put the flour into a mixing bowl with the salt, mix well then gradually add the water mixing with your fingers until the dough comes together to form a sticky dough. Knead the dough in the bowl until it feels firm and elastic, cover with a tea towel and leave to rest for 20 minutes. Divide the dough into eight pieces, shape into little balls, coat lightly with flour, roll into circles about 17cm diameter; flip the disc from hand to hand to stretch the dough.

Heat a heavy pan or griddle until very hot, don't add oil to the pan or the kitchen will be filled with smoke! Cook the bread one at a time, 30 seconds then turn over with a palette knife, cook for another 30 seconds and turn again, so the speckled surface is on top. As the bread puffs up, use a folded tea towel to flatten it down. Flip over again and repeat with the other side. Lift out of the pan, place on a tea towel and lightly brush with melted butter, keep warm while cooking the remainder, then serve immediately.

𝒥𝓇𝒾𝓈𝒽 WHITE SODA BREAD

Just out of the oven, butter melting on the slice, with strawberry jam, I'm back in my Mother's warm kitchen, with bread made every day: the best childhood memories.

[MAKES 1 LOAF]

450g strong white flour
1 scant level teaspoon bicarbonate of soda (bread soda), sifted
1 teaspoon salt
400ml buttermilk

Set oven to Gas 7/220°C and place a baking sheet in the oven to preheat. Mix the flour, soda and salt together in a large bowl. Add the buttermilk and mix really well until the mixture comes together. Lift out onto a floured surface and knead for a few minutes until smooth.

Place on the preheated baking sheet and make the traditional cross on the surface of the dough. Bake in the oven for 15 minutes, then reduce the heat to Gas 6/ 200°C and continue to bake for another 30 minutes. The bread will be baked when tapped on the base and it sounds hollow or use a digital probe: at 98°C it's fully cooked. Be careful to only use a 'scant level teaspoon' of bread soda. Too much and the bread will have a yellow tinge and taste of soda, which is not good. Otherwise it's the quickest and simplest bread to make.

the BALLYMORE INN SOURDOUGH GRANARY

We have always made granary bread and, over time, we have moved on to making a sourdough granary with a natural leaven – with no yeast. This bread has a wonderful flavour and texture: yes, there's time involved and you need to stay in tune with the fermentation process, but it's possible to make at home. There are four stages: the starter; the leaven; mixing the dough; baking the bread.

[MAKES 2 X 1KG LOAVES]

To make the starter, you'll need to work about 5 days ahead as the starter takes time to establish but once it is established you could make bread every day. So to make the starter mix 3 tablespoons white strong flour and 3 tablespoons granary or wholemeal flour with enough warm water to make a thick batter, mix well, cover with a kitchen towel and place in a cool place for 2-3 days. Check after two days to see if any bubbles have formed. If not, let it sit for another day. Once you have activity, it's time to start feeding the culture. Discard about 50% and replace the discarded portion with equal amounts of water and flour; it's best to do this at the same time every day. You'll notice when you add the flour and water that the volume of the starter will increase for several hours after feeding and then begin to collapse. Once a pattern is established your starter is ready for the next stage.

To make the leaven, mix 1 tablespoon of starter with 200g warm water plus 100g white flour and 100g granary or wholemeal flour, mix well and leave at room temperature overnight. In the morning it should be ready. To test it drop a spoonful into a bowl of warm water and wait a moment. If it floats it's ready, if not it needs more time to ferment. Set it aside in a warm place and check again in an hour. Once it passes the float test you are ready to mix the dough.

To mix the dough, weigh 600g of warm water and pour into a large mixing bowl, add 200g leaven, 500g white flour and 500g granary or wholemeal flour. Mix on a slow speed till well mixed, leave to rest for 40 minutes then add 20g salt and mix again. Set the dough aside for 3-4 hours in a covered container at room temperature then leave it in the fridge overnight.

To bake the bread, remove the dough from the fridge, divide into two loaves and leave it to rest on the work surface for about 40 minutes. Flour two bread proving baskets (banettones) really well, gather up each loaf and place in the baskets, cover and leave for 3-4 hours. When you are ready to bake the bread, set the oven to its highest setting possible, place two baking sheets in the oven to get really hot and a container of water to create some steam. Tip the dough from the baskets onto the hot baking sheets and, using a sharp knife or razorblade, slash the top of each loaf several times then bake for 50-55 minutes. Reduce the heat to Gas 6/200°C after 30 minutes. You can check the temperature of the bread with a digital probe; at 98°C it is ready. Remove from the oven and cool.

You can make bread every day once you have an established starter. If you are only going to make bread once a week then store the starter in the fridge and feed it once or twice a week. You'll find the banettone proving baskets in most kitchen shops. You can also get really good results baking the bread in a cast-iron casserole/Dutch oven. Preheat it and use the lid – this creates its own steam.

Chapter 4

FROM THE
garden

What's growing in your garden this year? Little or large, vast quantities or just a few pots of herbs, whatever you can manage, it's always worthwhile. Why just grow grass (that you have to mow) when you can pick the best tasting tomatoes right outside your door. Here are a collection of recipes featuring the best that summer has to offer. When you have the best tasting tomatoes, don't miss the tomato and bread soup; or a simple burger with delicious homegrown lettuce and sweet and sour onions; smoky aubergines with chargrilled steaks; the delicious West Cork buffalo halloumi is perfect with fresh coriander vinaigrette; creamy blackcurrant fool with crunchy biscuits and lemon cake with lemon balm syrup. There is no better time to enjoy the fruits of the garden, and to eat really well.

the BALLYMORE INN TOMATO and BREAD SOUP

This is the perfect way to use a glut of summer tomatoes - it's silky smooth and really delicious, a sublime French recipe. It's soothing, unalloyed comfort food, and we served this at the wedding of our daughter, Clare.

[SERVES 6-8 /45 MINUTES /EASY]

2kg ripe vine tomatoes
100ml olive oil
6 cloves garlic, chopped
½ teaspoon dried chillies
few sage leaves
salt & pepper
2-3 slices good quality bread

to serve
drizzle of aged balsamic & some basil oil (see page 11)

Chop the tomatoes roughly, removing the hard central core, but keeping the seeds and skins.

Heat a large, heavy pan with the olive oil, garlic, chilli and sage, simmer for 3-4 minutes to allow the garlic, sage and chilli to flavour the oil. Tip in all the tomatoes, season well and cook gently for about 30 minutes.

Tear up the bread and just add it in to absorb the juices – don't add too much bread. Serve with a drizzle of balsamic & basil oil.

While well-ripened summer vine tomatoes are ideal, I've been known to leave the not so well-ripened tomatoes in a warm sunny spot for a day or two and you'd be surprised how they improve. So don't let the lack of perfect tomatoes stop you, it's the best, most flavoursome vitamin boost you can imagine.

ROSEMARY *sauté* POTATOES

Sautés, as we call them, are a really popular menu item. The secret is that they are shallow fried, not parboiled, not deep fried and cooked to order.

[SERVES 4 /20 MINUTES /EASY]

4 tablespoons sunflower oil
8 medium potatoes, peeled and diced
sprig of rosemary
knob of butter
salt and black pepper

Heat the oil in a large heavy pan. When really hot, add the potatoes and sauté for a few minutes on a high heat. Reduce the heat and continue cooking until the potatoes are just soft and golden brown, about 15 minutes. Add the garlic (don't add too soon, as it will burn before the potatoes are cooked), and the rosemary, a knob of butter and season well.

GRILLED FLATBREADS *with* SLICED STEAK *and* BABA GHANOUSH

The delicious smoky flavour of the grilled aubergine purée makes this perfect for summer eating. Take your time to get that deep smokyness into the aubergine.

[SERVES 4 /40-50 MINUTES (INCLUDING BREAD TIME) /EASY]

grilled flatbreads (page 54)

4 x 150g dry-aged Irish sirloin steaks
salt & black pepper
olive oil
pinch of cayenne
pinch of smoked paprika

baba ghanoush
2 large aubergines
2 tablespoons tahini
2-3 cloves garlic, chopped
2 tablespoons olive oil
juice of 1 lemon
salt & black pepper
1 pomegranate, deseeded

To prepare the flatbread: mix the bread dough according to the recipe (see page 54), set aside. Season the steaks with salt, black pepper, oil, cayenne & paprika and set aside.

To give the baba ghanoush that smoky flavour, you need to blacken the aubergine skin on the barbecue or over a gas flame. Push sturdy metal skewers into the aubergine lengthways, set over the flame or barbecue, cook turning occasionally, until charred all over, and the aubergine is soft & tender – this will take 20-30 minutes. When cool enough to handle, remove the skin and roughly chop the flesh into a bowl. Stir in the tahini, garlic, oil, lemon juice and seasoning, and mix well, using a spoon to break up the pieces a bit more. Stir in half of the pomegranate seeds and spoon the mixture into a serving dish. Sprinkle the remaining pomegranate seeds on top, set aside.

To finish the dish: Divide the flatbread dough into four equal pieces and roll out into circles 2-3mm thick. Heat a griddle pan or barbecue; cook the flatbread for 3-4 minutes on each side, keep warm. Cook the steaks on the griddle pan or barbecue for 3-4 minutes for medium rare, rest for 5 minutes and slice. Serve the flatbread with the sliced steak and baba ghanoush.

CHARGRILLED IRISH BEEF BURGER *with* MELTED CHEDDAR

Nothing beats a good burger on a summer's day... to create the best burger, use freshly minced good-quality Irish beef. You will need some fat in the mix for flavour, about 15% – this amount is essential for juiciness. Cook the onions ahead to a caramelised, golden brown colour, for the final flavour.

[SERVES 4 /30 MINUTES PLUS SOME TIME TO COOL THE ONIONS /EASY]

1 tablespoon sunflower oil
1 large onion, finely chopped
pinch of dried chilli flakes
2 cloves garlic, chopped
700g minced Irish beef
salt & black pepper

sweet & sour red onions
2 red onions, finely sliced
2 tablespoons red wine vinegar
2 tablespoons golden caster sugar

4 burger baps (see page 49)

toppings
4 slices mature Irish cheddar
4 slices Serrano ham
frilly lettuce to serve
2 vine tomatoes, sliced
4 tablespoons tomato relish (see page 12)

To prepare the onions: Heat the oil in a medium pan and sauté the onions till well caramelised, 6-8 minutes. Add the chilli flakes and garlic, remove the mix from the pan to a large bowl and cool completely. Add the beef and generous seasoning, mix well and shape into four burgers, then store in the fridge till ready to cook. Mix all the ingredients for the sweet & sour onions together and set aside.

Chargrill or barbecue the burgers until fully cooked, check temperature 75°C, add a slice of cheese to each burger for the last 2-3 minutes, cover and the cheese will melt very quickly, or you could put them in the oven for 2-3 minutes until the cheese melts. Place the slices of Serrano on the grill or barbecue at the same time to crisp, and the burger buns to toast.

Put some lettuce on each bun base and top with a couple of slices of tomato, add some tomato relish, sweet & sour onions, the burger, crispy Serrano and bun tops, skewer each to hold it together and serve with lots of napkins!

FRIED WEST CORK BUFFALO HALLOUMI *with* TOMATO *and* AVOCADO SALSA

This is best eaten outside, in the warm company of sunshine on a fine summer's day, with lots of good bread on hand to mop up the dressing.

[SERVES 4 /30 MINUTES /EASY]

2 x 200g West Cork buffalo halloumi cheese
4 tablespoons well-seasoned flour, with a pinch of cayenne
2-3 tablespoons olive oil

tomato & avocado salsa
8 vine tomatoes, chopped
2 avocados, peeled, chopped
2-3 shallots, diced
1 red chilli, finely chopped
1 tablespoon capers, drained
juice & zest of 2 limes
2 cloves garlic, chopped
2 tablespoons fresh coriander, chopped
4-5 tablespoons olive oil
salt & black pepper

Slice the halloumi cheese into 16 slices, coat each slice in the seasoned flour. Mix the tomatoes, avocados, shallots and chilli together in a salad bowl. In another small bowl, mix the capers, lime juice & zest, garlic, coriander, olive oil and seasoning, and mix well. Add half of the dressing to the tomato & avocado salsa, and mix well together.

When you're ready to serve, heat a large heavy pan, add the olive oil and fry the slices of halloumi until golden brown on each side, serve straight away on warmed plates with the remaining dressing poured over and the salsa on the side.

FROM THE GARDEN [68]

GRILLED PORK CUTLETS *with* APPLE *and* RED ONION SALSA

I find it is best to buy the pork on the bone for flavour - I like to buy the full rack of pork with the chine bone off. The butcher will prepare this for you, and then you can slice them very easily into individual cutlets, and freeze what you don't need for another day. Marinading the meat gives extra flavour, whilst the Highbank syrup gives lots of sweet oomph! to the salsa.

[SERVES 4 /30 MINUTES PLUS MARINATING OVERNIGHT /EASY]

4 Irish pork cutlets

marinade
2 tablespoons olive oil
juice of a lemon
few sprigs of sage
2-3 cloves garlic, chopped
salt and black pepper

apple & red onion salsa
2 crisp apples, diced (not peeled)
2-3 cloves garlic, chopped
4 tablespoons olive oil
1 small red onion, finely chopped
1 red chilli, finely chopped
2 tablespoons Highbank Orchard Syrup
dash of cider vinegar
handful of chopped parsley
Salt and black pepper

Highbank Orchard Syrup is a delicious Irish-made syrup made from organic apples. If it's unavailable, use maple or date syrup.

Start the marinade a day ahead if possible: mix all the ingredients together and pour over the pork chops in a deep dish. Cover and leave in the fridge overnight, two nights is even better to flavour and tenderize the pork. To cook, mix all the salsa ingredients together and taste for a good balance of sweet and sour. Add more vinegar or apple syrup as necessary, set aside.

Grill or barbecue the pork for 3-4 minutes on each side until fully cooked, season as they cook and serve with a spoonful of the salsa.

DUNCANNON HAKE *with* GREEN CHILLI *and* LIME DRESSING *and* CUCUMBER SALAD

Serve with a glass of chilled rosé wine and you have summer on a plate. This technique for frying the fish won't let you down: just let the pan get very hot before putting the fish in, skin-side facing up. Adding the knob of butter when the fish is almost finished accentuates the lovely caramel colour that gives the contrast with the white flesh, and gives the dish its professional sheen.

[SERVES 4 /30 MINUTES /EASY]

---

4 x 180g fillets of hake, cod or plaice
salt & black pepper
olive oil
knob of butter

green chilli & lime dressing
2 green chillies
3-4 cloves garlic, chopped
finger piece of ginger, peeled & chopped
2 teaspoons sugar
rind & juice of 1 lime
125ml sunflower oil
salt & black pepper
3 tablespoons Greek-style yogurt

cucumber salad
1 large cucumber, with some of the skin removed, seeded and diced
1 small red onion, finely sliced
salad leaves
juice of half a lime,
salt & black pepper
olive oil

Starting with the dressing, chop the chillies - if you like the dressing extra hot keep the seeds. Place the chillies, garlic, ginger, sugar, rind and juice of the lime in the processor and whiz for a minute, then slowly add the oil and seasoning. Place the yogurt in a bowl, stir the chilli mixture through the yogurt and set aside for serving.

Season the fish well and drizzle with olive oil. Heat a heavy-based pan until very hot, add about a tablespoon of oil to the pan and cook the fish, skin side up. When the fish is just golden brown, add a knob of butter and cook for another minute, turn the fish and finish the cooking; now the fish will have a perfect caramel colour and a delicious butter flavour.

Mix the cucumber salad ingredients together in a large salad bowl, serve with the fish and the dressing on the side.

LEMON CAKE *with* LEMON BALM SYRUP

Everybody loves a freshly baked lemon cake, and when you have lemon balm available in the garden in the summer, well there's no better time to make it! You can replace the lemon balm with lemon thyme or, if the herbs aren't available, then lemon syrup is also fine.

[SERVES 10-12 /30 MINUTES PREP PLUS 1 HOUR BAKING /EASY]

200g butter, room temperature	**lemon balm syrup**
200g caster sugar	2 tablespoons sugar
100g self raising flour	handful of lemon balm leaves,
100g ground almonds	finely chopped
3 eggs, beaten	juice & rind of 1 lemon
rind of 1 lemon	

Set oven to Gas 4, 180˚C and line a 1kg loaf tin with non-stick baking paper.

To make the cake, in an electric mixer beat the butter and sugar together till white and creamy. Add half of the flour and ground almonds, mix well together, then add the eggs and the remaining flour, ground almonds and lemon zest. Spoon the mixture into the prepared tin and bake for 45-50 minutes, or until a skewer inserted in the centre comes out clean. Cool in the tin. Meanwhile make the syrup by putting the sugar, lemon balm, lemon juice and rind into a small pan, heat gently till the sugar dissolves. Simmer for a few minutes, then remove the cake from the tin and drizzle with the syrup.

BLACKCURRANT FOOL *with* ORANGE *and* ALMOND TUILES

This is a menu favourite in midsummer, when there are lots of blackcurrants ready for picking in our garden – simple and utterly delicious. In winter you can make the fool with frozen blackcurrants, so freeze any spare ones and then, when the days are short and cold, you can take it out of the freezer, and have the taste of midsummer in midwinter. Think of it as stored-up sunshine.

[SERVES 6 /30 MINUTES PREP /EASY]

350g blackcurrants
175g sugar
whipped cream (same weight as the fruit when cooked)
2 tablespoons hazelnuts, toasted and chopped

6 tall glasses for serving

To cook the blackcurrants, place in a heavy saucepan and cover with the sugar. Place pan over a low heat and cook till the fruit bursts, about 5-6 minutes. Purée the fruit then sieve and weigh. When the purée has cooled, add an equal quantity of softly whipped cream - if you wish, reserve a teaspoon of the purée for the base of each glass before you add the cream. Top up each glass with the purée and cream mixture, sprinkle with chopped hazelnuts and serve with orange & almond tuiles (see page 78).

RICH CHOCOLATE POTS *with* HONEYCOMB

A little pot of heaven – smooth chocolate, but with a crunchy surprise.

[SERVES 8 /30 MINUTES PREP PLUS A FEW HOURS TO SET/ EASY]

---

8 x 150ml individual serving dishes

600ml cream
300g dark chocolate, chopped
½ teaspoon vanilla extract
2 eggs
8 teaspoons honeycomb, chopped (recipe page 154)

Heat the cream to just below boiling point, pour the hot cream into the food processor, add the chocolate and blitz for a few seconds until you have a smooth cream, then add vanilla extract and eggs and mix well again.

Place a teaspoon of the honeycomb into each serving dish, then pour over the chocolate mixture. Place the dishes in the fridge to set. Serve with extra honeycomb, lemon & sugar biscuits (see page 78) and a chocolate curl.

To prepare chocolate curls, melt 100g dark chocolate and pour on a smooth surface to cool. When the chocolate is set, but still pliable, use either a vegetable peeler or a pastry knife to shave off curls. Store in an airtight box until needed.

PISTACHIO MERINGUES *with* LEMON CURD *and* SUMMER BERRIES

Our meringues change with the seasons: mango and passion fruit in the autumn; cranberry and orange in winter; chestnut and chocolate for Christmas; but by far the most popular we make is pistachio with summer berries. The remaining lemon curd will keep well in the fridge for a couple of weeks, and is delicious on hot toast.

MERINGUES

[MAKES 8 MERINGUES /A LITTLE EFFORT]

---

4 egg whites
250g golden caster sugar
100g pistachio nuts, finely chopped

Set the oven to Gas 2, 150°C and line a baking sheet with non-stick baking paper. Place the egg whites in a very clean, dry electric mixer bowl, whisk the eggs whites until stiff then keep the mixer running and add the sugar slowly until the mixture is stiff and glossy. Place eight generous spoonfuls of the mixture onto the lined baking sheet, sprinkle each one with a little of the chopped pistachio nuts and bake for 70 minutes. Cool on the tray.

LEMON CURD

grated rind and juice of 2 lemons
90g butter
90g golden caster sugar
2 eggs, beaten

Place the rind and juice, butter and sugar in a heatproof bowl, place over a pan of simmering water and stir until the butter has melted. Add the beaten eggs and continue stirring for about 15 minutes until the mixture is thick. Leave to cool and store in the fridge until needed.

to serve
250ml cream, whipped
3 tablespoons lemon curd
450g mixed strawberries, raspberries & blueberries
200ml caramel sauce (recipe page 192, but omit the passionfruit)
mint leaves

To assemble the meringues, mix the whipped cream and lemon curd together, spoon the mixture onto each meringue, add the berries and drizzle with the caramel sauce. Decorate each one with a mint leaf and serve.

ORANGE *and* ALMOND TUILES

These perfect crisp biscuits are really useful to serve with so many desserts. Make a batch - the dough will keep well in the fridge, or frozen for a few months, and they can be baked then as you need them.

[MAKES ABOUT 40 /20 MINUTES PLUS CHILLING TIME /A LITTLE EFFORT]

375g caster sugar
120g flour
150g butter, room temperature
175g flaked almonds
rind & juice of 1 large orange

Mix all the ingredients together to a stiff paste and chill for a couple of hours. Line a large baking tray with non-stick paper. Set oven to Gas 3, 150°C.

Take a teaspoon of the mixture and roll it in your hand then flatten with a fork on to the baking sheet, allowing plenty of room for the biscuits to spread. Cook for 15-20 minutes – do this in batches. When the biscuits are deep golden brown, lift them with a palette knife and lay them over a long rolling pin to set into a curved 'roof tile' shape. They are very pliable when hot, but if they cool too quickly just return them to the oven for a minute to soften and continue to shape. Cool and store in an airtight container.

LEMON *and* SUGAR BISCUITS

These are delicious with any mousse-type dessert or just with coffee.

[MAKES ABOUT 25 /40 MINUTES /EASY]

100g soft butter
120g icing sugar
rind of 1 lemon
2 egg whites
120g plain flour

Line two baking sheets with non-stick paper. Cream the butter, sugar and lemon rind together, fold in the egg whites and flour. Chill the mixture for 30 minutes.

Set oven to Gas 4, 180°C. Spoon the mixture into a piping bag fitted with a 1cm plain nozzle. Pipe long finger strips of mixture onto the lined baking sheets. Sprinkle each one with a little extra caster sugar and bake for 12 – 15 minutes until golden. You may need to turn the trays during the baking for even cooking. Leave biscuits to cool for a few minutes on the baking sheets then transfer to cooling racks.

Chapter 5

YOU'RE invited...

Creating homemade dishes - yes it's a lot of work but, it's also a wonderful treat. Now for most of us, conversation, sharing, and good food provides a refuge from the stressful world we live in, so this is our reward for all the work! Here are good crowd pleasing dishes, most can be prepared ahead and the flavours will actually improve on keeping a day or two in the fridge. Enjoy delicious pork rillette or creamy hummus over drinks or pre-dinner. A dish of Penang beef or Kashmiri chicken has the wow! factor, and who wouldn't long for a bowl of comforting Irish stew at end of a wearing day.

A simple cup of tea with a neighbour is elevated to a joyous occasion with the cranberry and orange cake, and family and friends will delight in your endeavours, thereby making every effort worthwhile.

CHICKEN LIVER PATÉ *with* PISTACHIO NUTS *and* PLUM RELISH

This has been on our menu from day one in the Ballymore Inn. It is one of those signature dishes our customers love, and today it remains the most popular item in the restaurant. This is great party food, served with slices of sweet brioche, with the tartness of the plum relish balancing the richness of the bread and the pâté.

[SERVES 8-10 /50 MINUTES /A LITTLE EFFORT]

1 x 2kg loaf tin lined with cling film

225g chicken livers
225g butter, room temperature
1 tablespoon brandy
black pepper
50g pistachio nuts, toasted

Trim the chicken livers of all membrane. Heat a large pan and add 50g of the butter and gently sauté the livers until fully cooked, with no traces of pink. Place the liver in a food processor. Add the brandy to the pan and flame, then add all remaining sediment to the processor and pulse for a few seconds. Add the black pepper and remaining butter, and continue to process until the mixture is smooth. Taste for seasoning: if using salted butter it may not need seasoning. Pour the mixture into the lined tin and sprinkle the top with pistachio nuts. Cover with cling wrap and leave overnight in the fridge to set.

You'll find it easier to slice the paté if you dip the knife into hot water between slicing.

To serve, slice the pâté. Serve with salad leaves, the plum relish and toasted brioche (see page 50).

PLUM RELISH

10-12 plums, stones removed & chopped
225g sugar
125ml red wine vinegar
small cinnamon stick

Place everything in a saucepan and simmer the lot until the plums are reduced to a pulp. Taste and adjust the sweet sour balance with more sugar or vinegar as required.

PORK RILLETTE

This 'potted pork' is really useful. Traditionally served with lots of good crusty bread, and robust red wine, French wine makers remain convinced that the high fat content helps to slow down alcohol absorption. Anyways, it tastes great.

[MAKES AT LEAST 12-15 FOR A PASS AROUND STARTER OR PARTY FOOD /30 MINUTES PREP & 3 HOURS COOKING /EASY]

2 kg Irish pork belly, skinned & deboned
2 whole bulbs of garlic, peeled
bunch of thyme, bay leaf & sage
sea salt, thyme and bay leaves to garnish

Set oven 150°C, Gas Mark 3. Cut the pork into long strips and pack into an earthenware or other ovenproof dish. Add the garlic and herbs, and season very well. Add just enough cold water to cover, cover tightly and cook in the oven for about 3 hours or until really tender.

Remove from the oven and spoon everything into a sieve or colander over a bowl to collect the juices. When cool enough to handle, pick out the meat pieces and place on a board. Remove the herbs and shred the meat using two forks, don't be tempted to use the food processor – it won't give you the correct texture. Taste for seasoning, then pile the pork onto a serving dish and pour over the remaining cooking juices. Sprinkle with some sea salt. Garnish with extra thyme & bay leaves. It will keep well in the fridge for a few days and is best served not too cold from the fridge.

GOUGÈRES

This is the classic party canapé, and a tasty cheese morsel worthy of the best glass of bubbly to pair with it. If you can't get Gruyere, then an aged Irish farmhouse cheese, such as Coolea, will work equally well.

[MAKES ABOUT 40-50 BITE SIZE PASTRIES /40 MINUTES /EASY]

125ml water
125ml milk
100g butter
generous pinch of cayenne
pinch salt
1 teaspoon sugar
150g plain flour
4 eggs, beaten
180g plus 2 tablespoons, finely
   grated Gruyere cheese
egg wash (1 egg yolk mixed
   with a pinch of salt and a
   tablespoon milk)

Set the oven 180°C, Gas mark 4. Line two to three baking sheets with nonstick paper. Heat the water, milk, butter, cayenne, salt and sugar together till the butter has melted. Stir in the flour and cook over the heat for a few minutes until dry and sandy.

Remove from the heat, stir in the eggs, beating well until the mixture becomes glossy and smooth, then add the 180g cheese and continue stirring until well mixed. Put the paste into a piping bag fitted with a 1cm plain nozzle. Pipe small mounds on to the baking sheets. Brush with egg wash and lightly mark the tops with the back of a fork, then sprinkle over the rest of the cheese. Bake in the pre-set oven for 20 minutes. Serve warm.

HUMMUS *with* WARM FLATBREAD

This recipe is proof that some of the best tasting things in life are the simplest to make.

[SERVES 8-10 /SOAK THE CHICKPEAS A DAY AHEAD, 20 MINUTES PREPARATION AND 1½ HOURS COOKING TIME /EASY]

400g dried chickpeas

2 generous tablespoons tahini

4-5 cloves garlic, chopped

sea salt

1 teaspoon ground cumin

juice of 3 limes

olive oil to garnish

Put the chick peas to soak for 24 hours in three times their volume of water as they will double in size. Rinse the chick peas under cold water, put them in a saucepan, cover well with cold water and place over a high heat. Bring to the boil, reduce the heat to medium and cook for 1 hour and 30 minutes or until very tender. Drain, keeping some of the liquid in case you need to thin down the purée. Process to a smooth paste with the tahini, garlic, salt, cumin and lime juice. If the purée is too thick, add a little of the cooking liquid. Taste for seasoning – it may need more salt or lime juice. Spoon into a serving bowl and drizzle with olive oil. Serve with lots of warm flatbread, (recipe page 54).

IRISH STEW *with* CAPER *and* PARSLEY DRESSING

There's no better comfort food than Irish Stew, the original of all the braised meat dishes. If you have to prepare the meat it's a little time consuming, so sometimes I use a leg of lamb to save time, but the traditional cut is shoulder or neck – they'll be cheaper, and have more flavour. The caper and parsley dressing is crucial.

[SERVES 8-10 / 1 HOUR PREPARATION PLUS 1½ HOURS COOKING TIME / EASY]

3kg neck or shoulder of lamb, boned (keep the bones), well trimmed and diced
bouquet of thyme, parsley and bay leaf (tied together with string)
2 large onions, finely chopped
salt & black pepper
4-5 carrots, chopped
3 small white turnips, chopped
4-5 leeks, chopped
8–10 potatoes, peeled and chopped
150g cabbage, finely chopped
finely chopped parsley and dash of Worcestershire sauce

Place the meat in a large saucepan cover with cold water, bring to the boil, drain and rinse the meat. In a fresh pot place the lamb, the bones, herbs, onions, seasoning, carrots, turnips and leeks, cover with cold water and simmer for an hour. Then add in the potatoes and cook for a further 25 minutes. For the last 5 minutes, add in the cabbage. Remove the bones and herbs before serving. Stir in the chopped parsley and Worcestershire sauce. Top each bowl with a spoonful of the dressing.

caper and parsley dressing
2-3 cloves garlic, 3 handfuls
  parsley, some basil
2-3 teaspoons capers
2-3 anchovy fillets
1 tablespoon wine vinegar
1 tablespoon Dijon mustard
200ml olive oil.

Blend all the dressing ingredients in the food processor and serve in a small bowl.

fiery FISH STEW

This is a great dish for a gathering. It is especially convenient as you can make the tomato base ahead of time, which will also allow the flavours to mingle and develop.

[SERVES 10 /40 MINUTES PREPARATION AND 15 MINUTES COOKING TIME /EASY]

tomato base

125ml olive oil

2 large onions, finely chopped

3 leeks, finely chopped

4-5 cloves garlic, chopped

2 tablespoons fresh ginger, chopped

1 teaspoon turmeric

100ml tamarind liquid

1 teaspoon dried chilli flakes

3-4 green chillies, cut in half lengthwise, retain the seeds & stem

4-5 curry leaves

250ml fish stock or water
3 x 400g cans chopped tomatoes
salt & black pepper
coriander & extra olive oil to garnish

the fish
allow 180g per person, and choose any combination of fish – hake, monkfish,
  prawns, mussels etc (keep refrigerated until ready to cook)
extra olive oil and seasoning

Make the tomato base: heat the olive oil in a large shallow pan, add the onions and sauté gently for 3-4 minutes. Add the leeks, garlic and ginger and continue to cook for another 2-3 minutes. Stir in the turmeric, tamarind, dried and fresh chillies and curry leaves, then add the stock and tomatoes. Season and bring to the boil, reduce the heat and simmer for 5-6 minutes. Set aside until just before you are ready to serve. The fish will cook very quickly. Shell and skin the fish, chop into chunks, not too small, and add the fish to the hot tomato base, allow to simmer gently until the fish is fully cooked, and check seasoning. Serve in deep dishes with a drizzle of olive oil and chopped coriander, lots of good bread or a large bowl of basmati rice.

If you are using fresh mussels, allow 4-5 per person, scrub each one really well and remove the beard. Discard any that remain open when tapped. Heat a glass of white wine in the base of a shallow pan, tip in the mussels, cover the pan and steam for 3-4 minutes, until they open, they are now cooked. Remove from the pan and add to the stew just before serving. Remove half the shells if you wish, and discard any mussels that don't open. Also add the cooking liquid to the stew for extra flavour.

CHINESE *slow roast* SHOULDER OF PORK

This is a definition of simplicity, for whilst it takes time, it takes precious little actual work, leaving you free to relax whilst it cooks away in the oven. It's a great way to feed a few friends, simply get everything ready and then let everyone make their own lettuce wraps at the table. It's delicious to eat and won't break the bank.

[SERVES 8-10 /OVERNIGHT TO MARINATE AND 4½ HOURS COOKING /EASY]

3kg boneless shoulder of Irish pork, skin removed
3 tablespoons sugar
3 tablespoons salt

1 whole bulb of garlic, cut in half
Few pieces ginger
2 red onions, peeled and roughly chopped

glaze
3 tablespoons honey
1 teaspoon sea salt
3 tablespoons soy sauce

to serve
round lettuce leaves
Basmati rice

A day ahead, lift the pork into a large dish, mix the sugar and salt together and rub this all over the pork. Leave in the fridge overnight.
The next day rinse the pork and pat dry. Heat the oven to 180°C, Gas 4. Line a roasting tin with foil - this will save a bit of washing up!
Place the pork on the foil in the roasting tin, add the garlic bulb, ginger pieces and red onion, gather up the foil around the meat, then add about 200ml water. Close the foil package, place in the hot oven and roast for 4 hours, check occasionally that there are plenty of juices around the meat; this is tenderising the meat during the cooking. While the pork is cooking make the pickles (see overleaf).
After about 4 hours, take the pork from the oven and remove the foil. Turn the oven up to 200°C, Gas 6. Mix the glaze ingredients together and pour this over the top of the pork. Put back into the oven for 20-25 minutes until the skin is dark golden and glazed.

CHINESE PICKLES

pickled cucumber & carrot

2 cucumbers

2-3 carrots

2 tablespoons golden caster sugar

3 tablespoons rice vinegar

1 red chilli, finely chopped

dipping sauce

1 tablespoon golden caster sugar

2 tablespoons rice vinegar

2 tablespoons soy sauce

1 bunch scallions, finely chopped

1 red chilli, finely chopped

3 cloves garlic, finely chopped

1 tablespoon ginger, finely chopped

Half the cucumber lengthways and scoop out and discard the seeds, cut cucumber into half moons. Mix the cucumber with half the sugar, vinegar and chilli. Set aside in a serving bowl. Slice the carrots on a mandolin or finely chop. Mix with the remaining vinegar, sugar and chilli. Set aside in another bowl. Mix all the dipping sauce ingredients together.

To serve cut the pork into chunks and let everyone make their own lettuce wraps filled with pork, rice, cucumber and carrot pickles and dipping sauce.

PENANG BEEF *with* FRESH GREEN CHUTNEY

Make this a day or two ahead and the flavours will settle and improve, and it can be kept in the fridge. The tamarind adds a slightly sweet-sour flavour to curries. It's sold two ways, in blocks of pulp which needs to be mixed with warm water and strained to remove the hard black seeds, or in jars as a concentrated paste.

[SERVES 8-10 /1 HOUR PREPARATION AND 1½ HOURS TO COOK /A LITTLE EFFORT]

2-3 tablespoons oil
2-3 large onions, finely chopped
3kg shoulder/chuck Irish beef, well trimmed, cut into finger size strips

spice paste	spices
3 cloves garlic, chopped	1 tablespoon coriander seeds
2 tablespoons fresh ginger, chopped	1 tablespoon cumin seeds
1 tablespoon lemongrass, chopped	1 tablespoon turmeric
3 red chillies, chopped	
rind & juice of 2 limes	100g peanuts, roasted & chopped
2 teaspoons sugar	2 x 400g cans coconut milk
100ml tamarind liquid (see note)	1 X 400g can chopped tomatoes
half can anchovies	salt & black pepper

Start with the onions: in a large pan heat a tablespoon of the oil and brown the onions really well. If they are browning too quickly, add a splash of water and continue cooking (you don't need more oil). When the onions are browned, transfer to a large deep casserole.

Sauté the beef in the same pan with the remaining oil. Don't overcrowd the pan. Transfer the beef as it browns to the onions in the casserole dish.

Next blend the spice paste: place all the ingredients in a processor and whiz for a minute. Remove and add to the beef and onions. Then, in a small pan, roast the coriander and cumin seeds, grind in a coffee/spice grinder and add to the casserole with the turmeric, peanuts, coconut milk, tomatoes and seasoning, cover and cook gently for 1 hour 30 mins or until the beef is tender. Taste for seasoning: you want a good balance of flavours – hot, sour, sweet and salty – garnish with chopped fresh coriander, extra red chilli and peanuts.

To serve: this curry goes well with basmati rice or flatbread (see page 54) and it goes especially well with fresh green chutney (see overleaf for recipe).

fresh green chutney
250ml Greek-style yogurt
2 tablespoons mint
2 tablespoons coriander
2 green chillies, chopped
salt

To make the chutney place the yogurt in a bowl. Put the herbs, chillies and salt in the processor with 1 tablespoon of the yogurt. Whiz to a paste, then stir the mixture through the remaining yogurt in the bowl and taste for seasoning.

KASHMIRI CHICKEN CURRY

This is a lovely, fragrant, creamy curry. Buy whole chickens, skin and cut into portions or just buy the portions. All curries are dependent on lots and lots of well browned (but not burnt!) onions, as this gives body and flavour to the sauce. You can double up the recipe, and it keeps well for 2-3 days in the fridge or you can freeze it. This is great party food: everyone loves a good curry.

[SERVES 8 /40 MINUTES PREPARATION PLUS 50 MINUTES COOKING /EASY]

2-3 tablespoons oil

3 large onions, finely chopped

2 teaspoons coriander seeds

2 teaspoons cumin seeds

2 teaspoons fennel seeds

6 cloves garlic, chopped

thumb size piece of fresh ginger, chopped

4 red chillies, chopped (no need to remove the seeds)

2 teaspoons turmeric

125ml Greek-style yogurt

2 x 400g cans of chopped tomatoes

juice of 1 lemon

2 teaspoons sugar

half cinnamon stick

4-5 cardamom pods

1 teaspoon black onion seeds

2 x 1.5 kg chickens, skinned
  and chopped into portions

salt and black pepper

dash of cream

If you are using whole chickens use the carcass to make some quick stock. Cover with cold water, chopped onion, peppercorns, bay-leaf and simmer. Then if you need some stock to dilute the sauce it will be ready and keep any left over, it's just about the most useful item to have in the fridge.

Start with the onions: heat a large pan, add a tablespoon of the oil and sauté the onions. It's best not to rush it - just let them caramelise gently, this is leisurely cooking! In another pan heat the coriander, cumin and fennel seeds until just roasted. Tip the seeds into a coffee/spice grinder and whiz until well ground, add the spices to the pan of well-browned onions, and cook together for a minute or two. Add in the garlic, ginger, chillies and turmeric. Stir in the yogurt and cook for another minute or two until well absorbed.

Add the tomatoes, lemon juice, sugar, cinnamon stick, cardamom pods and onion seeds. Let the sauce simmer for a few minutes. Season the chicken well. Heat the remaining oil in another pan and brown the chicken. Now add the chicken to the sauce. Cover and simmer for 40 mins until fully cooked. Keep an eye on the sauce and if it is too thick dilute it with chicken stock or water. Before serving taste for seasoning, you want a nice balance of flavours. Add a little cream and a bit more lemon juice if it needs it. Serve with basmati rice, naan bread (see page 48) and a handful of chopped coriander. Add some extra red chilli if you like. This date and yogurt chutney is also a winner with the curry.

---

date & yogurt chutney

2 tablespoons dates, chopped

3 tablespoons desiccated coconut

2-3 tablespoons Greek-style yogurt

2-3 scallions, finely chopped

Pinch of chilli powder

salt and pepper

Mix together and serve.

COCONUT, LIME *and* PECAN ICE CREAM

This is an ice cream from our vegan menu, delicious with the hot chocolate pudding.
(see overleaf for recipe).

[SERVES 10 /20 MINUTES, PLUS FREEZING TIME /EASY]

2x 400ml cans of coconut milk
200g golden caster sugar
Juice & rind 1 lime
100g pecans, toasted & chopped

Mix the coconut milk, sugar, lime juice, rind and pecans together. Tip the mixture
into an ice cream maker and whisk until set. Store in the freezer until ready to use.

If you are not using an ice cream maker, pour the mixture into a bowl and freeze.
Two or three times during the freezing process, remove the bowl from the freezer
and stir really well. This will prevent ice crystals forming.

HOT CHOCOLATE *and* SALTED CARAMEL PUDDINGS *with* COCONUT, LIME *and* PECAN ICECREAM

This is a real chocolate and caramel treat, with the irresistible yin-yang push-and-pull of the salt and the caramel.

[SERVES 10 /45 MINUTES PLUS 4 HOURS IN THE FRIDGE /A LITTLE EFFORT]

10 x 200ml mini pudding moulds

200g butter plus extra for buttering
 the moulds
200g dark chocolate
200g golden caster sugar
4 whole eggs & 4 egg yolks
200g plain flour
10 large teaspoons of cold caramel sauce
cocoa for dusting

caramel sauce
100g butter
250g golden caster sugar
250 ml cream
Pinch of sea salt

Brush the moulds thickly with soft butter. Melt the chocolate with 200g butter in the microwave on a low setting. Set aside.

Whisk the sugar, eggs and egg yolks together till thick, creamy and doubled in size. Stir in the melted chocolate and butter mixture, then fold in the flour until well mixed. Place a dessertspoon of the mixture in each mould, dot a teaspoon of the caramel sauce in the centre, then cover carefully with more mixture until the moulds are filled to about 1cm below the rim. Leave in the fridge for a minimum of 4 hours before baking.

To cook, set the oven to 200°C, Gas mark 6, place a metal tray in the oven and cook the puddings for 13 minutes. Remove from the oven and leave to stand for two minutes before turning out on to serving plates. Dust with cocoa and serve with the coconut ice cream (see previous page).

To make the caramel sauce: melt the butter in a heavy based pan, add the sugar and simmer for about 5 minutes until you have a golden caramel colour. Stir in the cream and continue to cook until thick and smooth. Add the pinch of sea salt, allow to cool completely. Leftover sauce will keep in the fridge for several weeks.

CRANBERRY *and* ORANGE CAKE

Who said that inviting some-one round to the house has to be a big deal?

Tea by the fire, and a slice of good cake, sounds like an ideal way to keep in touch.

[SERVES 8-10 /1 HOUR /EASY]

18cm cake tin lined with
  non-stick paper

250g butter, room
  temperature
250g golden caster sugar
250g self raising flour
100g ground almonds
2 eggs, beaten
2 tablespoons Greek-style yogurt
Rind of 1 orange
100g dried cranberries
100g sultanas

orange glaze
2 tablespoons golden caster sugar
Juice of half an orange

Set oven to Gas 4, 180°C. In the mixer beat the butter and sugar together until light and fluffy, Then add the flour, almonds, eggs, yogurt and orange rind, and fold in the dried fruit. Spoon mixture into the prepared tin and bake in the hot oven for 40 minutes or until a skewer comes out clean from the centre of the cake. Remove from the oven to cool. To prepare the glaze, heat the sugar with the juice in a small pan until the sugar is dissolved, then drizzle over the cake while still warm. Allow to cool completely. Remove from the tin and peel off the paper.

Chapter 6

Hottest

BBQs

There's nothing we like better than cooking and eating outside, and at the first sign of settled weather we're off, because everything tastes better in the sunshine. To make sure it is as safe and enjoyable as possible, I've listed some BBQ thoughts overleaf, to keep in mind...

Be organised around your barbecue, have enough work space, work out a detailed plan, decide what you can prepare ahead.

Have everything in place and ready to go and remember: an extra pair of hands or two are really useful.

Light the barbecue before the guests arrive, as it adds to the atmosphere —barbecuing is theatre! Plus, you want the initial smoke to have burned off.

Have some food ready to offer the early guests – hummus, rillettes – then there's no rush and with the main barbecue dishes you can wait until you have the heat just right and ready for cooking.

The charcoal must be grey before you start to cook.

Stay with your barbecue, for best results and for safety's sake: that extra pair of hands can do the fetching and carrying.

Remove the meat/fish from the fridge 15 minutes before cooking, to lose their chill.

Control the proximity of the food to the coals. If you can, use a rack system with different heights and moveable grills, if not move the food around from hot patches to cooler parts at the edges. Even with a very basic barbecue, you can arrange the coals in a pile where you want the most heat, then in another area flatten out the coals and this becomes the cooler part.

Don't try to turn the food until it's well set and nicely browned. Use a digital probe to test for 'doneness'. If cooking steaks, start with the well done, then the medium and finally the rare, in this order. All the steaks are ready to serve at the same time. Check the probe – well done = 75°C, (this is also the cooked temperature for chicken or pork.) Medium-well steak = 60-70°C, medium = 55-60°C, medium rare = 50-55°C, rare = 45-50°C.

Allow the meat to rest for a few minutes before serving and season again. Never be afraid of bold fresh flavours at the barbecue, the outdoor atmosphere can take it and remember, as in all cooking, practice makes perfect.

BARBECUED DRY-AGED FILLET STEAKS *with* ASPARAGUS *and* PARSLEY DRESSING

We use dry-aged West Cork beef for the simple reason that good eating quality requires an inordinate amount of care: you need a skilled farmer, the animals need the finest grass and gentle care, and the task must be completed by a skillful processor. With our West Cork beef, we get all these factors. When all the elements come together, Irish beef is magic to eat: there is nothing else like it. It's worth noting, too, that grass-fed beef is full of CLA's – conjugated linoleic acids – which are very good for our health, and good beef also has the correct balance of omega 3s and omega 6s. In fact, the best Irish grass-fed beef should be thought of as a health food.

[SERVES 4 /20 MINUTES /EASY]

4 x 150g Irish fillet steaks	**parsley dressing**
salt	4-5 tablespoons olive oil
black pepper	4 cloves of garlic, chopped
balsamic vinegar	handful of parsley, chopped
olive oil	1 tablespoon sherry or red wine vinegar
approx 20 asparagus spears	2 red chillies, chopped finely
4 skewers	salt & black pepper

Season the steaks with a generous amount of salt, black pepper, a drizzle of balsamic and olive oil then set aside while you make the dressing. Heat the olive oil in a shallow pan, sauté the garlic gently till slightly coloured, remove from the heat, add the parsley, vinegar and chilli, then season to taste, spoon into a serving bowl and set aside.

Thread the asparagus tips onto the four skewers, brush the asparagus with a little of the parsley dressing and set aside to marinate.

Light the barbecue and allow enough time for the charcoal to turn grey. Cook the steaks to your liking - 3-4 minutes on each side for medium rare. The asparagus will also cook also in 3-4 minutes on each side.

Serve with a spoonful of the dressing. A dish of rosemary sauté potatoes (see page 61) would be a perfect accompaniment together with a bowl of salad leaves.

Note: The steaks and asparagus will also cook very well on a hot griddle pan.

SICHUAN LAMB KEBABS *with* CHAR-GRILLED LIMES *with* CARROT *and* CHILLI SALAD

Sichuan flavourings work surprisingly well with Irish lamb, so toast the peppercorns lightly to bring out their aromatic quality and to make the marinade especially vivid.

[SERVES 4 /40 MINUTES /EASY]

lamb marinade
2 teaspoons Sichuan peppercorns, toasted & crushed
2 tablespoons sesame oil
1 tablespoon soy sauce
1 teaspoon chilli flakes

700g Irish leg of lamb, deboned, well trimmed, cut into small cubes
2 limes, halved

Starting with the marinade, mix all the ingredients together in a bowl, add the lamb pieces and mix well together, thread the lamb onto metal or wooden skewers soaked in water, set aside for a few hours if possible.

To cook, heat the barbecue or griddle to hot, cook the lamb for a few minutes on both sides, at the same time grill the lime halves. Serve the lamb kebabs with the salad, some dipping sauce and a squeeze of grilled lime juice over each one.

CARROT and CHILLI SALAD

3-4 carrots, peeled, grated into fine strips
3-4 scallions, trimmed & cut into fine strips
1 red chilli, cut into fine strips

dressing
1 tablespoon sugar
2 tablespoons rice vinegar
2 tablespoons sesame oil
1 tablespoon mirin
1 tablespoon soy
1 tablespoon coriander, chopped
1 tablespoon scallions, finely chopped

To make the salad dressing heat the sugar and vinegar in a small saucepan until the sugar dissolves. Remove from the heat and add the sesame oil, mirin, soy sauce, coriander and scallions. Allow to cool. Mix salad ingredients together in a large bowl, spoon over half the dressing, mix well. Save the remaining dressing to use as a dipping sauce for the lamb.

Sichuan peppercorns are available in Asian stores and some supermarkets: toast them lightly to bring out their aromatic quality.

POACHED *and* BARBECUED CHICKEN

This is my favourite way to barbecue chicken as you capture all the flavour, but you have none of the worries of undercooked chicken.

[SERVES 6-8 /30 MINUTES TO PREPARE AND 2 HOURS TO COOK /A LITTLE EFFORT]

2 tablespoons olive oil

1 onion, quartered

2-3 celery stalks, chopped

1-2 leeks, chopped

2 carrots, chopped

1 garlic bulb, halved

1 tablespoon fresh ginger, chopped

1 glass of red wine

1 cinnamon stick

2 star anise

2 red chillies, halved

2 tablespoons honey

2 tablespoons soy sauce

salt & black pepper

1 x 2.3kg free-range Irish chicken

Start by heating a large saucepan over a moderate heat, add the oil and sauté the onion, celery, leeks, carrots and garlic together for a few minutes, then add in ginger, red wine, cinnamon, star anise, chillies, honey and soy sauce. Bring to the boil, reduce the heat and simmer for 2-3 minutes.

Season the chicken and lay it carefully on the bed of vegetables in the pan, top up with about a litre of water, cover the pan, and simmer gently for about an hour and a half, or until the chicken reaches 75°C using a digital probe.

Preheat the barbecue. Strain off about 200ml of the cooking liquid into a small pan and reduce over a high heat until it becomes thick and syrupy, remove the chicken from the pan onto a tray, brush the reduced liquid over the chicken, this now becomes the barbecue glaze. Cook the chicken on a moderate barbecue, turning occasionally until blackened all over. The remaining cooking liquid can be boiled up also and served as a sauce with the chicken. Discard the cooking vegetables.

Lift the chicken onto a carving board and serve with barbecued vegetables.

barbecued SEAFOOD SALAD

This dish is a great addition to any barbecue gathering because you can cook it ahead of time on the barbecue or on a medium-hot griddle pan, and then serve as a starter at garden temperature.

[SERVES 6-8 AS A STARTER /30 MINUTES TO PREP AND 10 MINUTES TO COOK /A LITTLE EFFORT]

garlic & lime dressing
2 tablespoons garlic confit (see page 11)
grated zest and juice of 2 limes
1 tablespoon honey
100ml olive oil
1 tablespoon coriander, chopped
salt & black pepper

16-20 fresh prawns, peeled
4 squid tubes, cleaned and cut into 1cm thick
  rings
8 large scallops, each cut into 2 discs,
  or 16 small scallops

tarragon aioli (see page 11)
mixed salad leaves to serve

seafood marinade
1 tablespoon fresh ginger, grated
1 teaspoon smoked paprika
1 tablespoon coriander, chopped
150ml sunflower oil
1 teaspoon honey
1 tablespoon rice vinegar
1 red chilli, finely chopped
Salt & black pepper

Start with the dressing, mix all the ingredients together in a bowl and set aside. Next mix the marinade ingredients together in another bowl. Make the tarragon aioli using the recipe from page 11, but replacing 2 tablespoons chopped tarragon instead of the watercress.

Thread the prawns onto 4 or 5 skewers, if using wooden skewers soak them in water for 30 minutes beforehand, lay the kebabs on a tray with the squid and scallops. Brush the marinade over each fish piece, then store the tray in the fridge until ready to cook.

Light the barbecue or heat the griddle to medium high, cook the prawns for about 1-2 minutes on each side. Cook the squid for about a minute on each side, wrap the fish in foil as it cooks to keep warm, grill the scallops for about 30 seconds each side.

To serve, arrange the seafood on a large warmed platter and serve with the tarragon aioli, garlic and lime dressing and salad leaves.

BOULANGERE POTATOES

This is a very useful recipe to cook in the oven and keep warm while you barbecue the meat. Use a mandoline to slice the potatoes the same size.

[SERVES 10-12 /20 MINUTES PREPARATION PLUS 45 MINUTES COOKING /EASY]

2 tablespoons olive oil
generous knob of butter plus extra to butter the dish
few sprigs of thyme
6-8 cloves of garlic, finely chopped
2 large onions, thinly sliced
salt & black pepper
12 large potatoes, peeled & thinly sliced
1 litre chicken stock

Set oven Gas 4/180°C. Heat the olive oil in a pan, add the knob of butter and sauté the thyme, garlic and sliced onions until just soft, season well. Butter a large baking dish, add a layer of potatoes, then the onion mix. Continue layering until all the ingredients are used up, finishing with a potato layer. Pour in the stock and bake in the preheated oven for 40-45 minutes or until the potatoes are soft and golden brown.

MONKFISH KEBABS *on* LEMONGRASS SKEWERS *with* GRILLED FENNEL *and* CHILLI

The monkfish and fennel can be cooked on the barbecue or griddle pan. Cook the fennel and chilli first, and keep warm while you cook the monkfish kebabs.

[SERVES 4 /30 MINUTES /EASY]

4 x 180g monkfish fillets, trimmed
8 lemongrass sticks, trimmed
salt and black pepper and olive oil
4 fennel bulbs, sliced into thick slices
4 red chillies
lemon & honey dressing (see page 139)
1 tablespoon chopped coriander
1 red chilli, chopped

Cut the monkfish into bite size pieces.
Thread the fish onto the lemongrass sticks, season well and drizzle with olive oil. Keep refrigerated until you are ready to cook. They can be made up a few hours ahead and the lemongrass will flavour the fish. Next brush the fennel slices and whole chillies with olive oil and season also – set aside. Make up the dressing, stir in the coriander and chilli, season to taste.

When the barbecue is ready, cook the fennel and chilli first – two to three minutes on each side. Remove and keep warm. Then barbecue the monkfish - make sure the barbecue is at its hottest;: if you are using charcoal it must be grey. Cook kebabs for 3-4 minutes without turning until nicely browned, then cook for 3-4 minutes on the other side, brushing the kebabs with a little of the dressing for the last minute or two. Serve with the fennel and chilli and remaining dressing.

char-grilled SUMMER VEGETABLES

This dish is best cooked on the barbecue, but a ridged griddle pan makes a good alternative, and will also give you the desired grilled appearance.

[SERVES 8 AS A SIDE DISH /30 MINUTES TO PREP PLUS 30 MINUTES TO COOK /EASY]

basil dressing
rind and juice 1 lemon
4 tablespoons olive oil
handful basil, chopped
salt & black pepper

2 aubergines, sliced into rounds
4 courgettes, sliced diagonally into ovals
3 red peppers, deseeded and quartered
2 fennel bulbs cut into quarters
3-4 red chillies
3-4 tablespoons sunflower oil
salt & black pepper
2 tablespoons Garlic confit (see page 11)
2 tablespoons Kalamata black olives

Only use olive oil for the dressing, where you are going to barbecue or char grill at high temperatures it is best to use a sunflower oil, as the olive oil will burn and develop a bitter taste

Mix the basil dressing in a bowl and set aside. In another large bowl mix the aubergines, courgettes, peppers, fennel and chillies together with the sunflower oil and seasoning. Char the vegetables on the barbecue or hot griddle for 4-5 minutes until lightly blackened all over. Place on a large serving dish. Pour over the dressing. Add the garlic and black olives to the dish. Leave to sit at room temperature for an hour before serving.

GREEN BEANS *with* HAZELNUTS *and* BLACK OLIVES

This is a great side dish for a barbecue: crisp, clean and fresh.

[SERVES 4 /20 MINUTES /EASY]

200g green beans, chopped
100g hazelnuts, toasted & roughly chopped
50g black olives, pitted & halved

garlic dressing
2 shallots, finely chopped
juice of a small orange
2-3 garlic confit (recipe page 11) or 2 garlic cloves, chopped
4 tablespoons olive oil
salt & black pepper

Blanch the beans, and mix together with the nuts & olives in a large bowl. In another small bowl mix all the dressing ingredients together, pour over the bean mixture while the beans are still warm. Toss together and transfer to a serving dish.

TABBOULEH *salad*

The secret to this lovely fresh salad is lots and lots of fresh parsley, all finely chopped by hand! Traditionally small salad leaves are served on the side, to scoop up the salad, used as if they were bread.

[SERVES 6-8 /20 MINUTES PREP TIME AND 1 HOUR TO SOAK /EASY]

300g bulgur wheat (cracked wheat)
juice & rind of 3 lemons
150g parsley, finely chopped
100g mint, finely chopped
5-6 scallions, chopped
150ml olive oil
salt & black pepper
lemon wedges to garnish

To make the salad, rinse the bulgur in cold water, drain, place in a bowl and cover with approx a litre of boiling water, cover with a tea towel and leave for an hour to soak.

Diced tomatoes and cucumber may also added to the salad, but only at the last minute, otherwise the salad will become too watery.

In the meantime, mix the lemon juice and rind, parsley, mint, scallions, olive oil and seasoning together in a large bowl. When the bulgur is well soaked, drain and squeeze to remove any excess water, add to the herb mixture and stir well. Taste for seasoning. Spoon onto a serving plate, garnish with extra lemon wedges.

Chapter 7

Sunday ROASTS

Here are ten of my favourite roasts that will please family, friends and neighbours alike. The idea is to cook, gather, eat and chat. Of course, it doesn't have to be Sunday - it can be any time of any day. What's really important is the occasion when family and friends share the joys, as well as the sadness, and there is no better place to do this than at the table - it's just a special time of the week. I'd like to help the next generation to value the importance of family meals, even very small children still 'eating purées' enjoy being included and sitting up with everybody. These dishes are to be enjoyed: they're not complicated and when you've had success with the roast, turn to 'The Tarts' chapter and bake a masterpiece to complete the meal.

BEEF POT ROAST

The great advantage with a pot roast is that you have two to three hours cooking time when it does not need your attention, which is ideal for Sunday activities: a walk, the match, the gym or maybe just a nap! And then: it's ready when you are. I prefer to use a shoulder cut for this long, slow cooking as it keeps nice and moist. Silverside or eye of the round are cuts from the leg and these are a little too lean for a really good flavourful pot roast.

[SERVES 8-10 /30 MINUTES PREP PLUS 2-3 HOURS COOKING TIME /EASY]

2 tablespoons sunflower oil
salt & black pepper
3kg Irish shoulder joint (chuck beef)
2-3 sweet potatoes, peeled & chopped
1 celeriac, peeled & chopped
3-4 red onions cut into wedges
3-4 leeks, chopped
2 whole bulbs of garlic, cut in half through the centre
sprig of thyme, sage & bay leaves, tied together
glass of red wine
200ml stock

Set oven to Gas 3/ 170°C. Heat the oil in a large heavy flameproof casserole, season the beef well and brown in the hot oil and transfer to a plate. Then brown all the vegetables in batches and set aside half the vegetables till later. Return the beef to the casserole with half of the vegetables and all of the garlic and the bunch of herbs. Add the wine and boil up for a minute, then add the stock, cover and cook in the oven for two and half hours.

Remove from the oven and lift the beef on to a plate. The vegetables by this time will be very soft – scoop up the vegetables and push through a strainer, and add the vegetable purée back into the cooking juices in the casserole to give a delicious richness to the final sauce.

Return the joint to the casserole with the reserved vegetables and cook for another 20-30 minutes until these vegetables are just cooked. This is a little more trouble but you will have a lovely sauce and vegetables that still have some bite.

Serve the beef sliced with the vegetables and the sauce. Some salsa verde (page 130) or fresh horseradish dressing (page 166) on the side is also very good with the pot roast.

HONEY ROAST RACK OF BACON *with* STIR-FRY CABBAGE, SHALLOT *and* MUSTARD SAUCE

This is our take on 'bacon & cabbage' - there is simply no better comfort food. Always cook extra as bacon is delicious served cold, with baked potatoes and some of our tomato chutney.

[SERVES 8 /30 MINUTES PREP & 2 HOURS COOKING TIME /EASY]

2-3kg rack of Irish bacon on the bone
1 large onion, chopped
2-3 bay leaves,
handful of peppercorns

glaze
2 tablespoons mustard
2 tablespoons honey

shallot & mustard sauce

2 tablespoons sunflower oil

knob of butter

4-5 shallots, finely chopped

1 tablespoon Dijon mustard

dash of tarragon vinegar

200ml chicken stock

125ml crème fraiche

salt & black pepper

3-4 scallions, finely chopped

stir-fry cabbage

2-3 tablespoons sunflower oil

2 teaspoons fresh ginger, chopped

500g cabbage, cut into fine shreds

knob of butter

salt & black pepper

Place the bacon joint in a large saucepan with the onion, bay leaves and pepper-corns, cover with cold water, bring to the boil, then reduce the heat and simmer for one and half hours.

While the bacon is cooking make the shallot and mustard sauce. In a medium saucepan heat the 2 tablespoons oil with a knob of butter, sauté the shallots gently for 3-4 minutes, but don't colour. Stir in the mustard, cook for a minute, add the dash of vinegar, and cook for another minute then stir in the stock and crème fraiche. Simmer for 3-4 minutes until you have a creamy consistency, taste for seasoning and set aside.

When the bacon is cooked, check the temperature with a digital probe, 75°C is ideal. Remove bacon from the saucepan and place on roasting tray. Set the oven Gas 7/220°C. Spread the mustard over the bacon and drizzle with the honey. Place in the hot oven and cook for 20-25 minutes until nicely glazed.

Just before serving, heat the oil together with the ginger and stir-fry the cabbage. Add a knob of butter and season. Reheat the sauce and add the scallions.

Remove the bones from the bacon and cut into slices. Serve with a bowl of the cabbage and the sauce to pass around.

INDIAN ROAST LEG *of* LAMB

I like to do this dish late in the year, when the lamb is mature enough to take a layer of spices, plus the yogurt has a tenderising effect on late-season lamb – start the recipe a day ahead.

[SERVES 8 /20 MINUTES PREP, PLUS MARINATE OVERNIGHT AND 1 HOUR COOKING /EASY]

1 leg of Irish lamb, boned, well-trimmed & butterflied (your butcher will do this)

marinade
2 teaspoons cumin seeds
2 teaspoons coriander seeds
1 teaspoon turmeric
pinch of chilli flakes
3-4 cloves garlic, crushed
1 tablespoon fresh ginger, chopped
salt & black pepper
3 tablespoons Greek-style yogurt

redcurrant sauce
glass of white wine
2 tablespoons redcurrant jelly
salt & black pepper

Lay the meat flat, skin side down, in a roasting tin. Toast the cumin and coriander seeds in a small pan until they are aromatic, then grind together in a mortar and pestle or coffee/spice grinder. Tip the powder into a bowl; add the turmeric, chilli, garlic, ginger, seasoning and yogurt and mix well together. Spread the mixture over the lamb, cover and leave in the fridge to marinate overnight.

To cook, set oven to Gas 6/200°C. Place the lamb in the preheated oven and roast for 45 minutes for just pink lamb, add another 10 -15 minutes for more well done, reduce the heat after 20 minutes to Gas 4/ 180°C. Remove the lamb from the oven and keep warm. Pour off the cooking juices and set aside.

To make the sauce – boil up the wine until reduced by half, add in the cooking juices plus the redcurrant jelly. Simmer together until the jelly is dissolved and the sauce is a nice consistency, taste for seasoning. Serve with pilau rice, and a dish of spicy roast butternut squash.

PILAU RICE

[SERVES 8-10 /25 MINUTES /EASY]

2-3 tablespoons sunflower oil	pinch of saffron
Knob of butter	1/2 cinnamon stick
2-3 onions, finely chopped	300g basmati rice
2-3 cloves garlic, chopped	450ml stock or water
1 teaspoon coriander seeds, crushed	salt & black pepper
1 teaspoon cumin seeds, crushed	

Heat the oil in a large saucepan, add the butter, sauté the onions and garlic together but don't allow them to colour. Stir in the coriander, cumin, saffron & cinnamon and continue to cook for another minute over a gentle heat, then stir in the rice and coat it well with spicy onion mixture. Add the stock or water, season well, bring to the boil, stir once, reduce the heat to simmer and continue to cook for 10-15 minutes or until just cooked. The liquid should be just about all absorbed. Transfer to a serving dish, garnish with crispy fried onions (optional) or black onion seeds.

ITALIAN ROAST STUFFED PEPPERS *with* BRAISED BLACK BEANS *and* PESTO

[SERVES 4 /40 MINUTES PREPARATION PLUS 2 HOURS COOKING /EASY]

braised black beans

200g black beans, soaked overnight

2 tablespoons olive oil

2 red onions, sliced

3 cloves garlic, chopped

1-2 red chillies, chopped

salt & black pepper

4 large or 8 small red peppers

20 approx, cherry tomatoes, quartered

2 tablespoons basil oil (page 11) or a few basil
  leaves

3 garlic cloves, finely sliced

4 anchovy fillets (optional), chopped

salt & black pepper

2 balls of West Cork buffalo mozzarella, torn
  into pieces

2 tablespoons hazelnut pesto (page 23)

Rinse the soaked beans well under a cold tap, then place in a saucepan and cover with cold water. Bring to the boil and simmer for about an hour or until just soft, drain. Heat the oil in another large pan and sauté the onion for 2-3 minutes. Add the garlic and chillies, then tip in the drained beans and combine well with the onion mixture. Season, then spoon the beans into a baking dish and add just enough water or stock to barely cover. Set aside while you prepare the peppers.

Set oven to Gas 6/ 200°C. Cut the tops off the peppers and remove the seeds - any trimmings can be added to the beans. Fill each pepper with the cherry tomatoes, basil oil or leaves, and garlic. Tuck some chopped anchovy into each one, season. Place the pieces of mozzarella on top, drizzle each pepper with a little extra olive oil, lift the peppers onto the dish of black beans and bake in the preheated oven for 40 minutes or until well cooked with slightly charred edges. Keep an eye on the liquid, topping up if necessary. Serve with a little pesto spooned over each one.

LEMON, THYME *and* GARLIC ROAST CHICKEN

It's a good idea to roast two chickens at a time, even for a smaller household, for then you have lots of options for the week ahead: pasta; soup; sandwiches; and the lovely Chicken & Mango Salad (page 28). If you are cooking roast potatoes with the chicken, omit the water and place them around the chicken with the garlic. Cook for 45 minutes or until cooked and golden brown, then remove from the roasting tin and keep warm. Add the water or wine to the tin and finish the sauce.

[SERVES 4 /1 HOUR 20 MINUTES COOKING /EASY]

2kg Irish free-range chicken
50g butter, room temperature
1 lemon, cut into wedges
bunch of thyme
1 large onion, peeled & sliced
2 whole garlic bulbs
olive oil
salt & black pepper
1 tablespoon redcurrant jelly

Set oven to Gas 6/ 200°C. To prepare the chicken, lift the skin carefully and spread the soft butter over each breast. Put the lemon wedges and thyme into the cavity, place the sliced onion in the roasting tin, put the chicken on top, and break the garlic bulbs into individual cloves - no need to peel – and place the garlic around the chicken. Drizzle with olive oil and season well. Add a splash of water to the tin and roast for 20 minutes.

Turn the oven down to Gas 4/180°C, top up the water and cook for another hour or until fully cooked. Check the juices run clear, not pink, at the thigh - or much easier and more accurate is a temperature probe at 75°C – then remove from the oven. Leave the chicken to rest for 15 minutes. Boil up the juices, mash the garlic into the sauce, add the redcurrant jelly, and simmer for a few minutes until the jelly is dissolved. Strain into a smaller pan, taste for seasoning and serve with the sliced chicken.

ROAST BELLY OF PORK *with* PAK CHOI *and* PINEAPPLE SALSA

You can always cook extra for another day as the pork is delicious cold, served in a good crusty roll with a spoonful of salsa.

[SERVES 6-8 /OVERNIGHT MARINATING PLUS 3 HOURS COOKING/EASY]

3kg belly of Irish pork, rind on, on the bone (ask the butcher to score it really well or use a Stanley knife)

spice mixture

1 teaspoon chilli powder
1 teaspoon ground coriander
1 teaspoon ground cumin
salt and black pepper
glass of wine
200ml stock
dash of balsamic vinegar

pineapple salsa

1 pineapple, peeled & finely diced
1 red pepper, deseeded and diced
1 tablespoon fresh coriander, chopped
2-3 scallions, finely chopped
juice of a lime
1 red chilli, finely chopped

pak choi stir-fry

3 heads pak choi, sliced
2 tablespoons oil
1 tablespoon fresh ginger, chopped
2-3 cloves garlic, chopped
salt & black pepper

Start a day ahead, place the pork on a dish, mix the chilli, coriander and cumin together and rub into the meat. Cover with foil and leave in the fridge overnight.

To cook, set the oven to Gas 6/200°C. Season the pork with salt and pepper, and place in the preheated oven to cook for 2 hours or until the crackling is formed, then reduce the heat to Gas 4/180°C, add the wine & stock and continue to cook for another hour, keep the liquid topped up during the cooking.

Meanwhile make up the salsa – mix all the ingredients together and taste for seasoning.

Remove the pork from the oven and keep warm. Pour off the excess fat and boil up the juices with a dash of balsamic.

Stir-fry the pak choi in hot oil, add ginger, garlic, seasoning and serve with the sliced pork, cooking juices and a spoonful of the salsa.

ROAST MONKFISH *with* POTATOES *and* SALSA VERDE

A simple Sunday dinner - the potato base can be par-baked in advance if it's more convenient, then cooked with the fish, 30 minutes before serving.

[SERVES 4 /PREP TIME 20 MINUTES, 45-50 MINUTES COOKING /EASY]

---

potato base

1kg potatoes, peeled and sliced thinly

3 tablespoons olive oil, plus extra for drizzling

3-4 anchovy fillets, chopped

4 cloves garlic, sliced

1 large onion, sliced

salt & black pepper

4 x 180g fillets monkfish, well trimmed

salsa verde

large handful flat-leaf parsley, chopped

2 cloves garlic, sliced

1 teaspoon capers

4 tablespoons olive oil

salt & black pepper

Set the oven to Gas 6/200°C. Place the sliced potatoes in a large roasting tin, combine the olive oil, anchovy and garlic together, then pour the mixture over the potatoes, add the onion and seasoning, Mix well. Cook in the oven for 20-25 minutes until the potatoes are nearly cooked.

Season the fish well and lay on top of the potatoes, drizzle with some extra olive oil, return the roasting tin to the oven and continue to cook for about another 20 minutes or until the fish is cooked and the potatoes are golden.

While the fish is cooking, blend the salsa ingredients together, taste for seasoning. Spoon a little salsa over each fillet before serving and the rest on the side.

You can use half sunflower and half olive oil for the salsa verde, if you find the olive oil on its own too overpowering.

ROAST RIB OF BEEF *with* FRESH HORSERADISH

This is our Sunday roast and every Sunday lunch we serve 80-100 portions of this delicious dry-aged West Cork beef in the restaurant. Try to find fresh horseradish to make the dressing, as it makes all the difference to the final dish.

[SERVES 6-8 /15 MINUTES PREP PLUS 1 HOUR 30 MINUTES COOKING /EASY]

3kg Irish rib of beef on the bone
1 tablespoon black peppercorns, crushed
2-3 red onions, chopped
4-5 bay leaves
sea salt

gravy
1 glass of red wine
125ml well reduced stock
2 tablespoons redcurrant jelly
1 tablespoon good-quality balsamic vinegar

horseradish dressing
3 tablespoons fresh horse-
    radish, peeled & grated
200ml crème fraiche
salt & black pepper

Allow the beef to come to room temperature. Set oven to Gas 6/200°C. Place the beef in a roasting tray; cover the fat with the crushed peppercorns. Add the red onions and bay leaves to the roasting tin and season well. Cook the beef for an hour, check the temperature with a digital probe: 60°C will be rare to medium, continue cooking to your preference – 75°C will be well done. Reduce the temperature to Gas 4/180°C for the remainder of the cooking.

At this stage you can add some potatoes to roast in the tray, seasoned and coated in olive oil. When the beef is cooked to your liking, remove from the oven, keep in a warm place loosely covered with foil for 20 minutes - this is important as it allows the juices to settle before carving.

Continue cooking the potatoes until golden brown. Remove from the tray and keep warm. Add the red wine and stock to the roasting tray, boil up with the juices and any sediment, and then strain into a smaller pan. Discard the onion and bay leaves, add the redcurrant jelly and simmer gently for 3-4 minutes until you have a nice consistency. Taste for seasoning and add the balsamic. Set aside. While the beef is cooking, mix all the ingredients together for the horseradish dressing; it improves with a bit of time for the flavours to develop.

Carve the beef, serve with the gravy, roast potatoes and the horseradish dressing.

SLOW ROAST SHOULDER OF LAMB *with* MIDDLE EASTERN RICE *and* LENTILS

This is not a quick, 'knock it together' dinner but, when you have the time for some leisurely cooking, you won't find anything more delicious or comforting.

[SERVES 5-6 /40 MINUTES PREP & OVERNIGHT MARINATE, PLUS 3 HOURS COOKING/ MODERATE]

1 shoulder of Irish lamb, on the bone, trimmed	**spice mix**
	2 tablespoons coriander seeds
1 cinnamon stick	1 tablespoon cumin seeds
250g basmati rice	1/2 teaspoon dried chillies
200g lentils, cooked for 10 minutes, rinsed and drained	1 tablespoon turmeric
	3-4 cloves garlic
2 large onions, sliced and coated in seasoned flour	1 tablespoon fresh ginger, chopped
200g baby spinach	2-3 tablespoons yogurt
1-2 tablespoons honey	salt & black pepper

Start by marinating the lamb a day ahead. Roast the coriander and cumin seeds together in a dry pan and grind in a mortar and pestle or coffee/spice grinder. Take half the mixture, plus half of the chillies, turmeric, garlic and ginger, mix well with the yogurt and some seasoning. With a sharp knife make slits on the lamb, spread the marinade over the lamb, wrap in foil and keep in the fridge overnight.

When you are ready to cook, set the oven Gas 4/180°C. Place the lamb, still wrapped in foil, in the oven and cook for 3 hours. While the lamb is cooking prepare the rice. Heat 2 tablespoons of oil in a large heavy saucepan, add the remaining spices, cinnamon stick, garlic and ginger, add the rice, stir to coat then add the lentils. Add just enough water or stock to cover, put a lid on the pot and cook slowly until the rice is just cooked, stirring from time to time. Keep rice warm.

Just before you are ready to serve, sauté the onions in hot oil and stir them through the rice and lentils, then stir in the spinach. When the lamb is almost cooked, peel back the foil and drizzle 1-2 tablespoons of honey over the lamb, then put back in the oven to brown well. Carve the lamb and serve with the rice and lentil mix.

Serve a bowl of yogurt mixed with olive oil, chopped fresh coriander and seasoning as a topping. A salad of chopped tomato, cucumber, pomegranate seeds, olive oil and lemon would be very good as a side dish.

ROLLED PORK BELLY *with* APPLE *and* APRICOT STUFFING

The belly of pork has just the best flavour. It's economical to buy and, because the meat is rich, you can serve smaller portions. You can also vary the stuffing: hazelnuts and mushrooms; chestnut and fennel; or the great old favourite: sage and onion.

[SERVES 6-8 /30 MINUTES PLUS 2 HOURS COOKING /MODERATE]

2kg Irish pork belly, boned, rind on, scored (ask the butcher to score it or use a Stanley knife)

stuffing
1 tablespoon sunflower oil
1 large onion, finely chopped
50g soft apricots, chopped
1 eating apple, grated
1 tablespoon flat-leaf parsley, chopped
3 tablespoons breadcrumbs
grated rind & juice of 1 small orange
salt & black pepper

1 onion, chopped into large pieces
1 glass of wine
1-2 tablespoon redcurrant jelly

Place the pork flat on a board, rind side down. Season the pork on both sides. Set the oven to Gas 6/200°C.

To make the stuffing, heat the oil in a frying pan and sauté the onions for 2-3 minutes. Tip the onions into a bowl and allow to cool, then add the apricots, apple, parsley, breadcrumbs, rind and juice of the orange, and seasoning, combine well together. Spread the stuffing over the flesh side of the pork. Roll the pork up and tie at intervals with string. Place the pork in a roasting tin and cook for about an hour until the crackling is well formed, then add the onion pieces and wine to the tin. Reduce the heat to Gas 4/180°C and continue cooking for another hour. Top up the wine, if necessary.

Check the internal temperature of the pork with a digital thermometer – 75°C is fully cooked, place the pork on a carving board, remove the string, and cover loosely with foil to keep warm.

Strain the cooking juices into a small saucepan, discard the onions and remove excess fat. Boil up the juices with the redcurrant jelly, and check seasoning. Serve with the sliced pork and a large bowl of stir-fried cabbage. To prepare the cabbage shred it very finely then stir-fry in hot oil for 2-3 minutes, flavour with chopped ginger and garlic, season well. Simple, delicious and economical too.

Chapter 8

Weekend COOK

Eleven relaxed recipes to make when you have a spare afternoon to spend in the kitchen for family or friends, including some Middle Eastern flavours, and the best pub pie...

ARDSALLAGH GOAT'S CHEESE *and* ONION TART *with* LEMON *and* HONEY DRESSING

A delicious savoury tart, and a great vegetarian dish. This will serve 10-12 people as a starter, or 6-8 people as a main course.

[SERVES 6-12 /40 MINUTES PREP PLUS 45 MINUTES COOKING /MODERATE]

1 x 28cm pastry case (page 178)

1 tablespoon olive oil
generous knob of butter
2 large onions, thinly sliced
few sprigs of thyme
4 eggs
375g crème fraiche
salt & black pepper
300g Ardsallagh goat's cheese

To pre-bake the pastry case, set oven to Gas 4/180°C and place a baking sheet in the oven. Line the pastry case with foil and baking beans/rice and

slide onto the hot baking sheet. Bake for 20 minutes, remove from the oven and carefully lift the beans out, return to the oven for 5 minutes or so, until the surface is dry to the touch. Remove from the oven and set aside.

While the pastry is cooking make up the filling. Heat the olive oil and butter in a large shallow pan, sauté the onions gently for about 20 minutes – keep the heat low. When they are just turning golden, add the thyme. Beat the eggs, crème fraiche and seasoning together.

Spoon onions into the pastry case, pour over the eggs and crème fraiche mixture, crumble in the goat's cheese, return to the oven and bake for 45 minutes, until just set. Serve warm.

LEMON *and* HONEY DRESSING

Keep this recipe in your head – it is great with so many dishes: chicken salads; pork kebabs; and it's really good served with the warm Goat's Cheese and Onion Tart.

[MAKES APPROX 250ML]

juice & zest of 2 lemons
2 tablespoons honey
200ml sunflower oil
salt & black pepper

Place the juice, zest and honey in the processor, add the oil slowly until the dressing thickens, season. The dressing will keep well in the fridge for a week. To serve with the tart, drizzle a little over each slice and add some salad leaves on the side.

HARISSA SAUCE

Make plenty of harissa and serve with grilled fish, steak, or barbecued chicken, or the monkfish and prawn overleaf – it will keep in the fridge for 3-4 days.

2 red peppers, seeded and cut into 4
2-3 chillies, stems removed
1 teaspoon ground cumin
1 teaspoon ground coriander
2-3 garlic cloves, chopped
300ml olive oil
1 tablespoon fresh coriander, chopped
juice of 1 lemon
salt & black pepper

Grill the peppers and chillies until both are well charred (this gives the harissa the special smoky flavour). Remove from the heat and, when they are cool enough to handle, remove the excess black skin from the peppers, place the chillies and peppers in the processor, together with all the other ingredients, pulse until all are well combined, check the seasoning and pour into a serving bowl.

BAKED COD *with* TOMATO, FENNEL AND ROAST PEPPERS

This is a foolproof dish, which is more about assembling ingredients than cooking. Make the base a day or two ahead, and the flavours will improve.

[SERVES 4 /30 MINUTES PREP PLUS 35 MINUTES COOKING /EASY]

tomato, fennel & roast pepper base
2-3 tablespoons olive oil
1 Spanish onion, thinly sliced
2 red peppers, roasted, skinned and sliced
1 fennel bulb, trimmed & sliced
3-4 garlic cloves, chopped
1 glass white wine
400g can chopped tomatoes
125ml chicken stock or water
2 tablespoons red wine vinegar
4-5 basil leaves, chopped
salt & black pepper

4 x 180g fillets of cod, skinned
1 tablespoon Parmesan
basil oil (see page 11)

To start with the tomato and vegetable base, heat the olive oil in a deep pan and sauté the onion slowly for 4-5 minutes then add the sliced peppers, fennel and garlic and continue to cook for another minute. Add the wine and continue to cook to reduce by half, add in the tomatoes, stock or water, vinegar, basil and seasoning. Allow the mixture to simmer gently for 10 minutes.

Set oven to Gas 4/180°C, season the fish with salt, pepper and a little extra olive oil. Spoon the tomato and vegetable base into a baking dish, lay the fish on top, sprinkle with Parmesan and place in the hot oven for 35 minutes or until the fish is just cooked. Serve with a drizzle of basil oil and good crusty bread.

MONKFISH *and* PRAWN TAGINE *with* HARISSA

Turn up the heat with this big bowl of Middle Eastern flavours. Ras el hanout is a Moroccan spice blend of up to 50 ingredients, while harissa is a very useful addition to a lot of dishes.

[SERVES 4 /45 MINUTES /EASY]

700g monkfish or other firm white fish,
   trimmed & cut into bite-sized pieces
12-16 uncooked prawns, peeled
salt & black pepper
olive oil
pinch of saffron

tagine base
2 tablespoons olive oil
2 onions, chopped finely
3-4 cloves garlic, chopped
1 tablespoon fresh ginger, chopped
1 tablespoon ras el hanout
400g can chopped tomatoes
juice of 1 lemon
1 teaspoon brown sugar
salt & black pepper

Season the fish with salt, black pepper, drizzle with olive oil and a pinch of saffron, set aside and keep refrigerated until ready to cook. To cook, starting with the tagine base heat the oil in a heavy shallow pan, sauté onions for a few minutes, then add the garlic, ginger and ras el hanout, and cook for another minute or two. Stir in the tomatoes, lemon juice, sugar, and seasoning, bring to boil, reduce the heat and simmer for 3-4 minutes, set aside. Make the harissa (see previous page).

When you are almost ready to serve, reheat the base, add in the fish and cook for 5-6 minutes, stirring gently from time to time - it's important not to overcook the fish. Stir in a spoonful or two of the harissa and taste for seasoning. Serve the remaining harissa on the side and a bowl of giant couscous (see page 146).

See page 139 for Harissa Sauce recipe.

INDIAN PRAWN CURRY

This is quite simple to prepare, but do try to marinate the prawns for a few hours, at least, or overnight if possible.

[SERVES 4 /SEVERAL HOURS MARINATING PLUS 27 MINUTES COOKING /EASY]

curry sauce
2 tablespoons sunflower oil
2 large onions, finely chopped
1 teaspoon ground cumin
1 teaspoon ground coriander
½ teaspoon turmeric
½ teaspoon chilli flakes
2-3 cloves garlic, chopped
1 tablespoon fresh ginger, chopped
2 tablespoons Greek-style yogurt
400ml can chopped tomatoes
1 teaspoon garam masala
salt & black pepper

2 tablespoons fresh coriander, chopped
1 red chilli, finely chopped
600g raw prawns, peeled

marinade
3 tablespoons Greek-style yogurt
2 green chillies, chopped
pinch salt

Place the prawns in a bowl, add yogurt, chillies and salt. Mix well and leave to marinate overnight in the fridge if possible.

To make the sauce, heat the oil and sauté the onions for about 10 minutes until golden brown. Stir in the spices and continue to cook for another 2-3 minutes. Add the garlic, ginger and yogurt, and mix into the spice mixture. Add the tomatoes and garam masala, then season well and simmer for 15 minutes.

Just before you are ready to serve, stir in the prawns and the remaining marinade, cook over a medium heat until just cooked through. Garnish with the chopped coriander and chilli, serve with naan bread (page 48) and basmati rice.

HAKE *with* MUSHROOM RISOTTO

You will need risotto rice – Arborio or Carnaroli - and after that the technique is very straightforward. For a vegetarian option, replace the fish with asparagus or courgettes in summer, butternut squash or pumpkin in autumn, radicchio cooked in red wine and chestnuts for midwinter.

[SERVES 4 /45 MINUTES /EASY]

knob of butter
1 tablespoon olive oil
2-3 shallots, finely chopped
80g wild mushrooms, chopped
salt and black pepper
pinch of saffron
200g risotto rice
450ml hot chicken or vegetable stock
1 tablespoon Parmesan, grated
4 x 180g hake fillets or other white fish, seasoned

to serve
rocket leaves for each plate
asparagus spears
olive oil
lemon juice

Heat the butter and olive oil together in a pan, sauté the shallots for a minute, then add the mushrooms - no need to colour. Season, then add the saffron and stir in the rice and continue stirring until well mixed. Now add in a quarter of the hot stock and stir until absorbed. Add the next quarter of stock and continue until all the stock is absorbed and the rice is just cooked and creamy. Stir in the Parmesan.

In another frying pan, heat a little more olive oil and butter and cook the hake for 3-4 minutes on each side. Serve hake with the risotto and a few rocket leaves on each plate dressed with a drizzle of olive oil and lemon juice.

FILLET OF BEEF MEDALLIONS *with* SWEET POTATO *and* SPINACH SAUTÉ

This is the date night dish - no expense spared!

[SERVES 2 /30 MINUTES /EASY]

2 x 200g dry aged Irish fillet steaks
salt & black pepper
balsamic vinegar
olive oil

sweet potato & spinach sauté
1 tablespoon olive oil
2 sweet potatoes, peeled & diced
2-3 cloves garlic, chopped
$^1/_2$ tablespoon fresh ginger, chopped
100g baby spinach, washed

topping
50g streaky bacon, diced
2 tablespoons crème fraiche
50g Cashel Blue cheese, crumbled

Cut each steak fillet into two medallions, season with salt, black pepper, balsamic and olive oil and set aside while you cook the sweet potato. Heat a tablespoon of olive oil in a pan, sauté the sweet potato, garlic and ginger over a medium heat for 5-6 minutes until just soft and nicely golden, set aside.

Now heat a small pan and cook the bacon until crispy, stir in the crème fraiche and heat for a minute or two. Add the crumbled cheese and just allow it to melt, then set aside while you cook the steaks.

Heat a heavy ridged pan and cook the medallions to your liking. Just before they are fully cooked, reheat the sweet potato, stir in the spinach and seasoning. Serve the medallions with the sauté, and a spoonful of the topping.

SPICY LAMB CUTLETS *with* GIANT COUSCOUS *and* SAFFRON YOGURT

Unlike regular couscous, giant couscous takes approximately 20 minutes to cook, and has a lovely nutty flavour.

[SERVES 4 /40 MINUTES PLUS MARINATING /EASY]

12 Irish lamb cutlets, well trimmed

marinade
2 teaspoons ground cumin
1 teaspoon turmeric
1 red chilli, chopped
2-3 cloves garlic, chopped
2 tablespoons oil
salt & black pepper

saffron yogurt
4 tablespoons Greek-style yogurt
generous pinch of saffron
1-2 cloves garlic, finely chopped
drizzle of olive oil
seasoning

couscous
2 tablespoons oil
1 red onion, thinly sliced
1 red chilli, chopped
200g giant couscous
600ml stock or water
salt & black pepper
100g baby spinach, washed

to garnish
extra chopped chilli & sprigs of mint

Starting with the lamb, mix the marinade ingredients together in a large dish, coat each cutlet and set aside for an hour to allow the flavours to develop. Next heat the oil in a deep pan and sauté the onion for a few minutes with the chilli. Add the couscous and continue to sauté for a minute or two, until it's well coated with onion, chilli and oil. Add the stock or water, seasoning and simmer gently until just cooked. Keep an eye on the liquid; it may need topping up. You can cook it ahead if it's more convenient and reheat. Stir in the spinach just before serving.

To cook the lamb, heat a heavy, ridged pan and cook the cutlets for 2-3 minutes on each side or to your liking. Mix the saffron yogurt ingredients together and taste for seasoning. To serve, spoon the couscous onto the plates, place the lamb on top and garnish with chilli and mint leaves and saffron yogurt on the side.

LAMB MEATBALLS BAKED *with* WEST CORK BUFFALO MOZZARELLA

We've become very attached to West Cork buffalo mozzarella, and not just in salads – we discovered it makes an excellent addition to lamb meatballs.

[MAKES ABOUT 30, SERVES 6 /60 MINUTES /EASY]

3 tablespoons olive oil

2 large onions, finely chopped

3-4 cloves garlic, chopped

2 red chillies, chopped

glass of red wine

2 x 400g can chopped tomatoes

1 teaspoon sugar

125ml stock or water

1 tablespoon balsamic vinegar

1 tablespoon basil, chopped, plus extra for serving

salt & black pepper

1kg Irish minced lamb

30g Parmesan, grated

200g West Cork mozzarella, roughly torn

Heat half the oil in a large pan then sauté the onions, garlic and chillies together until soft and the onions are lightly browned. Scoop half the mixture into a large mixing bowl and set aside to cool. To the remaining mixture in the pan, add the glass of wine, bring to the boil and reduce by half, then add the tomatoes, sugar, stock or water, balsamic, basil and seasoning. Bring to a gentle simmer for 10-15 minutes, set aside.

Add the lamb mince with the Parmesan and some seasoning to the cooled onion mixture, mix well together. Using damp hands, roll mixture into balls about the size of a walnut. If time allows, chill the meatballs for a few hours, this way they'll hold their shape better in the sauce.

Heat the remaining oil in another large pan and fry the meatballs in 2 or 3 batches until brown all over. Transfer to the simmering sauce using a slotted spoon and leave to simmer for 20 minutes or until the meatballs are cooked through.

Set oven to Gas 6/200°C. Spoon the meatballs and sauce into a shallow 2.5 litre baking dish, scatter over the torn mozzarella and bake for 15 -20 minutes until bubbling. Serve with some extra basil leaves and crusty bread – ciabatta is the best (page 53).

GUINNESS, STEAK and KIDNEY PIE

An archetypal winter warmer. You can make the pie filling in advance, if you wish, and can freeze it for up to 3 months.

[SERVES 6-8 /40 MINUTES, PLUS COOK-ING TIME /EASY]

3 tablespoons sunflower oil

2 large onions, diced

1kg Irish chuck/ braising steak, well-trimmed, cut into chunks

500g beef kidney, washed, trimmed of membrane & chopped

300g button mushrooms, halved

4-5 cloves garlic, chopped

250ml Guinness

125ml stock or water

1 tablespoon tomato puree

Never be tempted to use round steak (cut from the leg) for any slow braising dish as it will dry out during the long, slow cooking, but always choose a cut from the shoulder of beef for flavour and succulence.

a few sprigs of thyme

dash of Worcestershire sauce

1 teaspoon sugar

salt & black pepper

500g ready made all butter puff pastry

1 egg beaten to glaze

1.75 litre pie dish

Heat half the oil in a large pan and sauté the onions until golden. Transfer to a large flameproof casserole then add a little more oil and brown the beef and kidney in batches, transferring to the casserole as they brown. Sauté the mushrooms and garlic in the same pan, then add the Guinness, stock, tomato puree, thyme, Worcestershire sauce, sugar and seasoning, stir well and bring to the boil. Pour the sauce over the meat, cover and simmer gently for one and a half hours or until the meat is tender. Take off the lid for the last 30 minutes if the sauce needs to be reduced. Check seasoning and cool the filling completely.

To make up the pie, roll out the pastry on a lightly floured surface, then put the pie dish upside down in the centre and cut out a lid slightly larger than the top of the dish. Spoon the filling into the pie dish and brush the rim with beaten egg, lay the pastry lid on top and seal the edges. Make a small hole in the centre of the pastry to allow the steam to escape, then chill for 30 minutes. Set oven to Gas 6/200°C. Brush the surface with the remaining egg and bake pie for approximately 45-50 minutes until the pastry is golden and the filling is bubbling hot.

CUMIN *spiced* CHICKEN

When cooking this dish, the size of pan is hugely important: if it's too large, the cooking liquid will evaporate and you'll have very little sauce at the end of cooking time. If it's too small, then the flavours won't have room to mingle. Ideally, the pan should hold all the ingredients comfortably. Over time it is good to build up a variety of different sized pans; sauté pans with lids that are flameproof are the most useful.

[SERVES 4 /30 MINUTES PLUS COOKING TIME /EASY]

1 large Irish free-range Irish chicken
3 tablespoons olive oil
3-4 red chillies, chopped
4-5 cloves garlic, chopped
1 tablespoon cumin seeds, toasted
1 tablespoon flour
salt & black pepper
450ml stock or water

Start by cutting the chicken into 8 pieces. If you have the time, use the wing tips and backbone to make some stock. Set the oven to Gas 4/180°C. Heat a pan with a tablespoon of the oil, add the chillies and garlic and cook gently for a few minutes, set aside. Grind the cumin seeds in a spice grinder or mortar and pestle, then take half the cumin and add to the flour in a bowl with the seasoning and mix well. Add the chilli and garlic mixture to the remaining cumin in the mortar and pestle and mix to a paste.

Next coat the chicken pieces in the cumin-seasoned flour, heat the remaining oil in a large pan and brown the chicken on all sides. Add the spice paste and stock, mix well, cover the pan and cook in the oven for 40 minutes, until fully cooked: digital probe 75°C. Check the seasoning and serve the chicken with rice, alongside a bowl of mixed salad leaves.

Chapter 9

Christmas FARE AND Edible GIFTS

Following a very informal piece of consumer research with different age groups as to what they'd like to see included in the Christmas Chapter, the general consensus was that they wanted the traditional dinner, starter, soup, the roast and the pudding. They wanted the instructions to be clear, concise and to work! So here they are: a simple but delicious smoked salmon starter, a Thai-style wonton soup just to add a little spice to the day, a magnificent turkey roast, a pomegranate-glazed ham, a 60-year-old plum pudding recipe and some nice additions to the cheese plate, plus some very useful edible gifts, which, if you can organise the prep time, can prove to be a really cost-efficient way to manage your gifts...and who wouldn't love to receive a plum pudding or a pot of cranberry relish.

CHOCOLATE HONEYCOMB

We serve these as petit fours, and they make an ideal gift at Christmas.

[MAKES ABOUT 20 PIECES /40 MINUTES /EASY]

100 g caster sugar
4 tablespoons honey
2 teaspoons bread soda

200g chocolate, melted for coating

Mix the sugar and honey together in a pan and place over the heat – don't stir, just allow the mixture to turn golden. Remove from the heat, stir in the bread soda and turn the mixture onto non-stick paper to cool. When cool, break into pieces and coat in the melted chocolate, then allow to set.

CHOCOLATE and CARAMEL MACADAMIA NUTS

We serve these delicious treats with coffee - they would also make lovely gifts wrapped up in little packages.

[MAKES APPROX 50 /40 MINUTES /EASY]

3 tablespoons sunflower oil
175g macadamia nuts
150g sugar
125ml water
knob of butter
225g chocolate
150g icing sugar

Heat the oil in a large pan, add the nuts and cook gently until just golden brown. Remove from the oil and set aside. In another pan, melt the sugar over a medium heat. When it is just beginning to brown, carefully add the water and butter, cook the caramel for a minute and add the nuts. Coat the nuts with the caramel mixture then spread them out on a baking sheet covered with parchment paper to cool. Melt the chocolate in a large bowl on a low setting in the microwave, add the nuts and coat them with the chocolate. Spread the nuts on the baking sheet again, and leave in the fridge until the chocolate is set. Dust with the icing sugar and store in a cool, dry place.

You can melt the chocolate on a low setting in the microwave, stirring as it melts, but always be careful that it doesn't burn. Alternatively you can melt it in a bowl over simmering water, being careful that no water boils into the chocolate. Choose the chocolate that you like: we use Callebaut 53.7% dark chocolate drops which we find has a good balance of richness but is not too bitter.

CHOCOLATE BROWNIES

A little girl wrote on her plate, using the last of the chocolate, that these brownies were: 'the best'. Can't do better than that!

[SERVES 12 /45 MINUTES /EASY]

4 eggs
225g golden caster sugar
350g dark chocolate
225g butter
225g plain flour

Line a 26cm square tin with non-stick paper. Set the oven to Gas 4/180°C. Whisk the eggs and sugar together until thick and creamy. Melt the chocolate and butter together, fold into the mixture then very gently fold in the flour. Pour mixture into the lined tin and bake for 25 minutes – they should be slightly soft in the centre.

CHOCOLATE TRUFFLES

[MAKES ABOUT 45 TRUFFLES /45 MINUTES PLUS SETTING /MODERATE TO EASY]

600g dark chocolate
200ml cream
50ml rum
300g butter, room temperature

coating
250g dark chocolate, melted
300g cocoa powder

Melt the chocolate for the truffles on a low heat in the microwave. Boil the cream in a small saucepan and cool, and then stir into the melted chocolate with the rum. Whisk the butter until light and fluffy, stir into the chocolate mixture and mix well. Leave in the fridge till set. Take spoonfuls of the mixture, about 13g, shape into walnut-sized pieces. Melt the chocolate for the coating in the microwave as before. Using a skewer, dip each truffle in the melted chocolate, then leave on a tray lined with non-stick paper to harden in the fridge. To finish, coat truffles in the cocoa powder, store in a very cool place or keep in the fridge.

FLORENTINES

We introduced these delicious biscuits to the kitchen shop for Christmas, but found they stayed in production until after Easter!

[MAKES 16/ 45 MINUTES/ MODERATE]

50g butter
150g golden caster sugar
20g flour
130ml cream
100g hazelnuts, chopped

100g macadamia nuts, chopped
75g glace cherries, chopped
75g crystallised ginger, chopped
50g mixed peel, chopped

200g dark chocolate, melted to coat

Line a large baking sheet with non-stick paper and cook in two or three batches, or you can use special florentine tins, or shallow Yorkshire pudding tins also work very well, keeping them all the same size.

Set oven to Gas 5/190°C. In a saucepan, place the butter, sugar, flour and cream. Heat gently till the butter melts, stir well, then add the nuts, cherries, ginger and mixed peel. Place small scoops of the mixture onto the trays and bake for 10-12 minutes, moving the trays around during cooking to ensure they cook evenly. Cool slightly in the tins then cool on a tray. When cold, coat the underside with melted chocolate.

PECAN and COFFEE FUDGE

A perfect handmade gift - wrap up in cellophane and tie with a ribbon.

750g golden caster sugar

250ml liquid glucose

315ml cream

200g white chocolate, chopped

175g dark chocolate, chopped

250g pecans, chopped

75g butter

3 tablespoons Irel coffee or espresso

baking tin 32cm x 24cm x 3cm, lined with non-stick paper

Place the sugar, liquid glucose and cream in a heavy pan, stir well to mix all the ingredients, cook over a medium heat, stirring until the sugar is dissolved. Increase the heat and bring to the boil, stirring all the time, lower the heat slightly and cook without stirring until the fudge reaches 124°C (test with a probe or sugar thermometer), remove from the heat and mix in the chocolate, pecans, butter and coffee. Pour mixture into the lined tin and leave to cool, overnight if possible, but don't refrigerate. When completely set, cut into squares.

VANILLA SHORTBREAD

This is our Grandmother's original recipe, taken from a very old *Irish Press* newspaper cutting... we think it's the best!

[MAKES APPROX 15 PIECES /30 MINUTES /EASY]

225g plain flour
75g golden caster sugar
150g butter, room temperature
½ teaspoon vanilla extract

Set oven to Gas 3/160°C. Line a baking sheet with non-stick paper. Mix all the ingredients on a slow speed in the food mixer, until all is well mixed and forms a soft dough. Roll out on a floured surface, until 5mm thick, cut into finger pieces and carefully transfer to a baking sheet. Bake for 15 minutes, then turn the baking sheet and cook for another 15 minutes; the shortbread should remain pale and the under-side more golden. Remove from the oven and cool on the baking sheet.

CRANBERRY, ORANGE *and* GINGER RELISH

No Christmas table is complete without 'the cranberry'. There's no need to buy it, it's so simple to make and taste the difference! Make a few extra for the days after Christmas and to give as gifts.

[SERVES 20 APPROX /30 MINUTES /EASY]

2 x 350g bags fresh cranberries
400g sugar
juice & rind of a large orange
1 tablespoon finely grated fresh ginger
dash of port (optional)

Place all the ingredients in a shallow pan, and simmer over a gentle heat until the cranberries become tender, about 20 minutes. Cool and store in the fridge or pack into sterilised jars while still warm, cool then store for 2-3 weeks in the fridge.

traditional SEVILLE ORANGE MARMALADE

The season for making marmalade is very short as the Seville oranges are only available for 3-4 weeks after Christmas, so you need to watch out for them.

[MAKES 6KG /3 HOURS /EASY]

2kg Seville oranges, well washed
5.5 litres water
4.5kg sugar

12 jars
muslin bag
probe

Put the oranges into a large stainless steel saucepan with the water, place a plate on top to keep the oranges under the surface, bring to the boil and simmer for 2 hours. Drain and reserve the liquid - the reserved liquid should not be more than about 2 litres. Cut the oranges in half, scoop out the soft centres and place in the muslin bag with the pips and any juices, tie up the bag with string and place in the saucepan. Cut the peel finely, add to the saucepan together with the reserved liquid.

Warm the sugar in a moderate oven for 10 minutes, add the sugar to the saucepan and simmer gently till the sugar is dissolved. While the marmalade is cooking skim off the foam as it rises to the top then just before you finish cooking add a knob of butter to the pot and this will disperse the last of it. When the sugar is dissolved, increase the heat and boil until setting point is reached: 110°C on a digital probe or place a small amount on a cold plate and cool for a few minutes, if it wrinkles when you push it with your finger it is ready.

Allow marmalade to settle for 20 minutes. Meanwhile, wash the jars and sterilise them by placing in a moderate oven for 15 minutes. Fill the jars and cover while still warm then leave jars to cool.

This marmalade also works very well with frozen oranges,so buy extra as the season is so short and freeze in 2 kg. bags, you can then make it any time of the year, coming up to Christmas a pot makes a great welcome gift.

SPROUTS *with* TOASTED HAZELNUTS *and* CRISPY BACON

Keep the liquid to a minimum, the cooking time short and you'll avoid the dreaded overcooked cabbage flavour.

[SERVES 8-10/30 MINUTES/EASY]

1-2 tablespoons olive oil
100g Irish streaky bacon, diced
1kg brussels sprouts, trimmed, cut really finely
1 tablespoon butter
rind & juice of 1 orange
salt & black pepper
100g hazelnuts, toasted & roughly chopped
2 tablespoons pomegranate seeds

Cook the bacon ahead, then the sprouts can be quickly cooked close to the serving time. Heat the olive oil in a large shallow pan and cook the bacon till crispy. Remove from the pan and set aside.

Sauté the sprouts for a minute or two in the remaining juices. Add in the butter, rind and orange juice. Season, add back the bacon. Stir well, transfer to a warm serving dish and sprinkle over the hazelnuts & pomegranate seeds.

LEMONGRASS BROTH *with* SCALLOP WONTON

A great starter for the festive season. You can make the broth base well ahead, and it also freezes well.

[SERVES 12 /16 MINUTES COOKING PLUS RESTING /EASY]

broth base

3 litres chicken stock

3-4 lemongrass, finely chopped

2 tablespoons ginger, grated

3-4 cloves garlic, finely chopped

2 red chillies, finely chopped

dash of fish sauce

rind & juice of 2 limes

1 teaspoon sugar

salt & black pepper

24 wonton wrappers

12 large scallops

3 scallions, finely chopped

3 tablespoons fresh coriander, chopped

extra chopped red chilli

Place all the broth ingredients in a large saucepan, bring to the boil, reduce the heat and simmer for 5-6 minutes. Set aside for a few hours before you are going to serve the broth to allow the flavours to develop.

Clean the scallops, pull off the roe and trim; pat the scallops dry with kitchen paper otherwise the wonton wrappers will go soggy when they're filled. Lay the wonton wrappers out and put a scallop in the centre of each, wet the edge of the wrapper and press another wrapper on top - these will keep in the fridge for a couple of hours.

To serve, bring the broth to the boil, taste for seasoning: it should have a nice balance of hot, sour, sweet and salty. Adjust the seasoning as necessary, then carefully add the wontons and simmer gently for 8-10 minutes until the wontons are cooked. Put a wonton in each soup bowl and ladle over the broth. Garnish with scallions, coriander and chopped chilli.

DUNCANNON SMOKED SALMON *and* ROCKET SALAD *with* AVOCADO *and* FRESH HORSERADISH DRESSING

This is a lovely simple combination, and a great Christmas starter. We use Duncannon smoked salmon, but there are many excellent Irish producers - use the best quality you can find.

[SERVES 10 /20 MINUTES /EASY]

5 handfuls of rocket leaves
3-4 tablespoons olive oil
sprinkle of sea salt
juice of ½ lemon
4 ripe avocados, peeled and thinly sliced
700g smoked salmon, sliced
lemon wedges, to serve

horseradish dressing
2 tablespoons fresh horseradish, peeled & grated
8 tablespoons crème fraiche
Salt & pepper

Try to find fresh horseradish and make the dressing a day ahead for the flavours to develop, any leftover dressing will keep for the next roast beef dinner.

Mix the rocket leaves with the olive oil, sea salt and lemon juice. Divide the leaves between the plates and arrange the sliced avocado and smoked salmon on the salad. Mix the dressing ingredients together with plenty of seasoning and drizzle over the salad. Serve salad with extra lemon wedges and some treacle bread.

THE CHRISTMAS TURKEY with LEMON and THYME STUFFING

The festive bird is not nearly as difficult as it might seem. First, choose the best quality turkey you can find – the best weight is 5-6kg for 10-12 servings, plus left-overs. Calculate the cooking time at 15 minutes per 450G (1lb) and 15 minutes over but, best of all, use a digital probe to check that the meat in the centre of the breast or thigh joint (not the bone) has reached 75°C. Buy the probe when you buy the bird! Then leave it to rest, covered with foil and a towel, for up to an hour.

[SERVES 10-12 /MODERATE]

5-6kg turkey
large roasting tin
250g butter, room temperature
8-10 streaky rashers

lemon & thyme stuffing
180g butter, room temperature
1 large onion, finely chopped
2 lemons
300g soft breadcrumbs
5-6 tablespoons flat-leaf parsley, chopped
1 tablespoon thyme, chopped
salt & black pepper

gravy
2 glasses of red wine
250ml chicken stock
3 tablespoons redcurrant jelly
generous knob of butter
salt & black pepper

The stuffing can be made a day or two ahead and kept in the fridge – don't stuff the turkey until you are ready to cook and don't wash the turkey.

To make the stuffing, melt a tablespoon of the butter in a medium pan and sauté the onion gently for a few minutes but don't colour. Grate the zest of both lemons then juice just one. In a large bowl mix the breadcrumbs with the onion, zest and lemon juice, parsley and thyme. Add the remaining butter and mix thoroughly, season well. Set aside till you are ready to roast the turkey.

Set the oven to Gas 4/180°C. Sit the turkey on the roasting tray, put the stuffing in the cavity, but keep a couple of tablespoons back for the neck cavity. Sew it up or use skewers to seal the stuffing inside. Spread the butter over the breasts and cover with the streaky bacon, then cover the turkey with foil and place in the preheated oven. It is worth basting the turkey with the cooking juices every 45 minutes. A glass of wine can be added for the last hour; remove the foil also at this point to ensure the skin browns well. Check the temperature of the turkey is 75°C then remove from the oven and leave to rest for an hour.

To make the gravy, to the remaining pan juices, add the other glass of wine and boil up, stirring well to gather up the caramelised bits. Add in the stock and redcurrant jelly then simmer gently until well dissolved. Check the seasoning and strain into a smaller pan or gravy boat for serving.

POMEGRANATE ROAST HAM

The roasting ham fills the house with the amazing smells of Christmas. You can cook the ham 2-3 days ahead, and reheat it while the turkey is resting, removing any last-minute timing and cooking space worries.

[SERVES 10-12 /4 HOURS COOKING /EASY]

5kg approx. Irish ham joint
3 bay leaves
1 onion, chopped
1 tablespoon black peppercorns
1 cinnamon stick

for the glaze
3 tablespoons pomegranate molasses
3 tablespoons honey

Put the ham in a large, heavy based pan, add the bay leaves, onion, peppercorns and cinnamon. Cover the ham with cold water, bring to a gentle simmer and cook for about 3 hours, until it reaches 65°C. Lift the ham out of the cooking liquid, place on a board and, using a sharp knife, cut the skin away from the ham, leaving as much fat as possible.

Check ahead if the ham needs soaking. If so, leave soaking in cold water for 24 hours. In general, the curing is now quite mild and it's not necessary. If you are cooking the ham ahead, continue to boil until it reaches 75°C and is fully cooked, then you can just glaze it in the hot oven on the day. Keep the ham stock as it makes the best soup.

Heat the oven to gas mark 6/200°C. Score the fat, then mix the molasses and honey together and brush the glaze thickly over the surface of the ham. Transfer the ham to a roasting tin and roast 45-50 minutes, basting with the glaze in the tin once or twice. When the ham is 75°C, glossy and sticky, remove from the oven, and allow it to stand for 10-15 minutes, then slice and serve.

CHRISTMAS PUDDING *and* BRANDY BUTTER

This pudding has been served in our family each Christmas for at least the last 60 years. Our sister, Ann Marie, is the current custodian of the recipe and is very happy to share it so that it may be enjoyed for at least another 60 years. Each pudding will serve about 6-8.

[MAKES 3 X 1L PUDDINGS /1 HOUR PREPARATION 5 HOURS COOKING /MODERATE]

300g fine breadcrumbs
225g butter, room temperature
100g plain flour
$\frac{1}{2}$ teaspoon grated nutmeg
1 dessertspoon mixed spice
225g soft brown sugar
100g whole almonds, blanched & chopped
50g ground almonds
1 large cooking apple, peeled & chopped
1 small carrot, grated
225g raisins
100g mixed peel, chopped

325g sultanas
150g currants
100g cherries, quartered
juice & rind 1 lemon
1 tablespoon treacle
4 eggs beaten
scant teaspoon bread soda
1 tablespoon wine vinegar
generous measure brandy

Butter the 3 pudding bowls and cut 3 generous rounds of greaseproof paper to cover, you'll also need twine to secure the paper.

In a large mixing bowl, place the breadcrumbs and rub in the butter. In another bowl, mix the flour, spices and sugar together, then add to the butter and bread-crumbs. Add the almonds, apple, carrot, raisins, peel, sultanas, currants and cherries, mix well together. Mix the lemon juice and rind with the treacle and a tablespoon of warm water plus the beaten eggs, add to the mixture and stir really well. Now make a wish! If it's more convenient, you can leave it covered overnight. When you are ready to cook, mix the bread soda with the vinegar and add to the pudding mixture. Last, but not least, add the brandy. When everything is really well mixed, divide between the pudding bowls.

Cover with the greaseproof paper, make a pleat in the centre, this will allow for expansion during the cooking, now tie the paper firmly under the rim. Place the bowls in saucepan/s of boiling water one-third full and simmer gently for 5 hours, don't let it boil over the top or let it boil dry either. When the puddings are cooked, replace the paper top and store in a cool dry place until Christmas. They'll keep very well and improve with time - we often have the last one on St Patrick's Day. To serve on the day, reboil for 2 hours. Serve with brandy butter.

BRANDY BUTTER

100g butter, room temperature
100g icing sugar
6 tablespoons brandy

Mix the butter and sugar together in a food processor, then add the brandy drop by drop. Store in the fridge but serve at room temperature.

the CHEESE BOARD

The cheese selection completes the Christmas feast. Choose the cheeses you like - Stilton is, of course, the traditional choice served with a glass of port. Here is the recipe for our delicious cheese biscuits and quince paste.

THE BALLYMORE INN CHEESE BISCUITS

Delicious little oatmeal biscuits for a cheese board.

350g wholemeal flour
100g oatmeal
200g butter, soft
4 dessertspoon brown sugar
2 teaspoons baking powder
6 tablespoons water

Set oven to Gas 4/180°C. Mix all the ingredients, except the water, in a food processor, then add just enough water to form a dough. Roll out the dough, cut into small rounds and bake for 15- 20 minutes.

QUINCE PASTE

This has a lot of uses: not only is it a great addition to a cheese plate, but it's also delicious served with pâté and ham, or stirred into sauces for pork or chicken. It will keep for months in the fridge and makes a great gift too.

1kg quince, peeled, cored & chopped
1 vanilla pod, split
2 lemons, zest & juice
1kg granulated sugar, approx

Place the quince pieces in a saucepan, cover with cold water then add the vanilla pod and lemon zest. Bring to the boil, reduce the heat and cook till tender, about 25-30 minutes. Drain, discard the vanilla pod then purée the quince pieces in a food processor. Weigh the purée: whatever the weight is you need the same amount of sugar. Place the quince puree, sugar and lemon juice in a saucepan, cook over a medium heat stirring till the sugar is dissolved. Continue to cook over a low heat, stirring occasionally for approx 2 hours till it is very thick and has a deep orange pink colour. Pour the mixture into a shallow baking dish lined with parchment paper to cool. Store in the fridge wrapped in cling wrap. To serve, cut into squares and serve with cheese etc.

Chapter 10

TARTS, TREATS
and SWEETS

A homemade tart with buttery pastry is the perfect self–contained treat, a delectable indulgence and just about the most satisfying food to make and eat. Here are a selection of my easy- to- follow favourites to take you through the seasons. Pecan and honey for example for the dark mid-winter days, plum and almond for the golden days of autumn, raspberry for peak summer, coconut and blackcurrant to use up the surplus of garden produce, lemon for sheer perfection and the chocolate and orange for the very special occasion or a very special person. But the really great advantage of 'Tart' for dessert is it will be made well ahead so there's no last minute thinking about it or fussing. Display it on the counter top for everyone to admire and look forward to the treat ahead... so warm the oven, rolling pin and tart tins ready, and away you go.

THE BALLYMORE INN TART CASE

Every lunch and dinner in the restaurant we have a warm fruit tart, made with homemade pastry and filled whatever fruit is in season. The pastry is the key to success: we make it in batches, line the tart tins and freeze them. Here is the recipe for just one tart but, if you have the space and the tins, then it's worth doing more than one at a time.

[TO LINE 1 X 28CM X 3CM LOOSE BASED TART TIN]

250g plain flour
180g butter, cold, cut into cubes
75g icing sugar
2 egg yolks

Put the flour and butter in a large bowl and rub them together with your fingertips until the mixture resembles coarse breadcrumbs, or you can do this in the processor. Tip in the sugar, mix lightly, now work in the egg yolks until you have a smooth dough. Roll the dough into a ball, wrap in cling film, and chill for at least an hour (or up to 3 days).

Some of the tart recipes require the pastry case to be precooked before filling - check out the instructions on the individual recipes. To precook the pastry case, set the oven to Gas 4/180°C, line the tin with pastry and bake the pastry shell using non-stick paper and baking beans or rice to weigh it down. Place in the hot oven and bake for 20 minutes - keep a close eye on the edges, and cover if necessary to prevent over browning.

CHOCOLATE *and* ORANGE TART

This is our favourite chocolate tart. Silky smooth and the best is, it can be made a day ahead. Be careful to only use the juice of half an orange, too much and the filling will not set.

[12 SLICES /1 HOUR PREPARATION PLUS OVERNIGHT TO SET /MODERATE]

28cm pastry case, cooked (see opposite)

chocolate and orange filling
630ml cream
200g honey
450g dark chocolate, chopped into
  pieces
225g butter, cut into cubes
Zest 2 oranges & juice of half an orange

Heat the cream and honey together, stir in the chocolate, butter, zest and juice. When the mixture is smooth and the chocolate and butter are melted, pour the mixture into a bowl and allow to cool.

When the mixture is just tepid and beginning to thicken, pour it into the cooked pastry case and chill in the fridge overnight to firm up the filling. Serve with a bowl of orange segments, or blood oranges in season, drizzled with caramel sauce (see page 192, but omit the passion fruit pulp).

CHOCOLATE *and* PEAR TART

This combination is very good, especially over Christmas

[SERVES 12 /30 MINUTES PREPARATION, PLUS 55 MINUTES COOKING/ EASY]

28cm pastry case (see page 178)

6 conference pears, peeled & thinly sliced

100g butter, room temperature
100g golden caster sugar
100g ground almonds
2 eggs
50g amaretto biscuits
300g dark chocolate, melted

2/3 tablespoons apricot jam
squeeze of lemon juice

Set the oven 180°C/ Gas mark 4 Mix all the filling ingredients in a food processor and spoon the mixture into the pastry case. Arrange the sliced pears on top and bake for 50–55 minutes.

To glaze, heat the apricot jam together with the lemon juice and brush the tart with the warmed jam.

COCONUT *and* BLACKCURRANT TART

We use our homemade blackcurrant jam for this tart which is very good but you can use any favourite jam.

[SERVES 12 /30 PREPARATION TIME AND 45 MINUTES OVEN TIME /EASY]

28cm tart case, cooked (see page 178)

4 eggs
250g golden caster sugar
juice & rind of 4 limes
200g desiccated coconut
175g melted butter
3 tablespoons blackcurrant jam
icing sugar for dusting

Set oven 180°C/Gas 4. Beat the eggs and sugar together, add the lime juice and rind. Stir in the coconut and melted butter, and mix well. Warm the jam and spread over the cooked pastry case. Pour the coconut filling over the jam base and bake the tart for 45 minutes. Cool and dust with icing sugar.

PECAN *and* HONEY TART

This pecan tart is well up the list of favourites at the Ballymore Inn. Keep an eye during the cooking that the pastry edges don't over cook, you may need to wrap them in foil.

[12 SLICES /45 MINUTES PREPARATION PLUS 40 MINUTES COOKING /EASY]

filling

450g pecans, broken into small pieces

225g honey

180g butter

150ml cream

7 egg yolks

225g caster sugar

1 teaspoon vanilla extract

28cm tart case, cooked
(see page 178)

Set the oven to Gas 4/180°C and place a flat baking sheet in the oven to preheat. Toast the pecans in a dry pan for a minute or two, remove and set aside.
Make a syrup by putting the honey, butter and cream in a pan and heat gently until the butter has melted. Beat the egg yolks, sugar and vanilla together and stir in into the syrup. Arrange pecans on the pastry case. Pour the mixture over the pecans, carefully place the tart on the baking sheet and bake for 40 minutes.

TARTE TATIN

This French apple tart is traditionally made with puff pastry but I like it with our buttery pastry. Use the tart case recipe (see page 178) and roll out to about 20cm, then keep chilled until needed.

tart case recipe (see page 178)

filling
200g sugar
50g butter
12 granny smith apples, peeled, cored & cut into wedges

a heavy 20cm tatin tin or shallow sauté pan

Set oven to Gas 4/180°C. Add the sugar to the pan and cook over a medium heat till the sugar turns to caramel. Add the butter and then pack in the apples, tightly side by side, and continue to cook over the heat until the juices are dark caramel – you need it to be a rich caramel, dark as you dare.

Cover apples with the pastry and tuck in the edges. Place in the preheated oven and cook for 35-40 minutes. Remove from the oven and allow it to cool for 10 minutes. Put a large serving plate over the pan and flip the tart onto the plate, taking care as the hot caramel can ooze out. Serve warm.

SUMMER RASPBERRY TART

When the raspberries are in season there is no better way to celebrate summer. There are a few stages to this tart, but the advantage is that you can prepare the pastry and filling a day or two ahead and assemble on the day.

[SERVES 12 /2 HOURS PREPARATION, PLUS 40 MINUTES COOKING /MODERATE]

28cm pastry case, cooked (see page 178)

lemon crème patissiere
3 egg yolks
100g golden caster sugar
1 tablespoon plain flour
1 tablespoon cornflour
250ml milk
juice & zest of 1 lemon
50g butter

frangipane

85g butter, room temperature
85g golden caster sugar
85g ground almonds
rind of 1 lemon
1 egg

topping

100ml cream
5 x 125g punnets raspberries
4 tablespoons redcurrant jelly to glaze, or icing sugar to dust

To make the lemon crème patissiere, put the egg yolks and sugar into a bowl and whisk together until the mixture turns pale. Tip in the flour and cornflour and mix well. Put the milk and lemon zest into a saucepan and bring to the boil. Pour the boiling milk over the mixture in the bowl, whisking continuously until everything is smooth. Pour the custard back into the pan, place over a medium heat and simmer for 3-4 minutes, stirring continuously until it has thickened. Remove the pan from the heat and stir in the lemon juice and butter. Pour the custard into a clean bowl and cover the surface with cling film to stop a skin forming. Leave to cool, then put in the fridge until completely cold (it will keep in the fridge for 2 days).
Next make the frangipane – tip all ingredients into the processor and mix until everything is well combined (the frangipane will keep in the fridge for 4 days).

To assemble and bake, put a baking sheet in the oven and preheat the oven to Gas 4/180°C. Stir the crème patissiere until smooth and spread three quarters of it over the base of the tart case. Spoon the frangipane into a piping bag fitted with a smallish nozzle, about 1cm. (If you don't have a piping bag, spoon into a freezer bag, squeeze it into the end and cut off the tip. Pipe the lines of frangipane evenly over the custard. Don't worry about the gaps as the frangipane will spread during the cooking. Put the tart tin on the hot baking sheet and bake for 40-45 minutes, remove from the oven and allow to cool completely.

To make the topping, whip the cream, fold the remaining crème patissiere into the cream, then spread evenly over the frangipane and arrange the raspberries on top. Heat the redcurrant jelly in a small saucepan and brush the raspberries lightly to form a glaze, or just dust with icing sugar.

PLUM *and* ALMOND TART

The secret here is the amaretto biscuits in the filling!

[SERVES 12 /30 MINUTES PREPARATION PLUS 55 MINUTES COOKING /EASY]

28cm pastry case (see page 178)

filling
100g butter, room temperature
100g golden caster sugar, plus 2-3 tablespoons for sprinkling
100g amaretto biscuits
100g ground almonds
2 eggs
10-12 plums, cut in half, stones removed

Set the oven to 180°C/Gas 4 and place a baking tray in the oven to preheat. Make the filling in the processor by mixing the butter, sugar, biscuits, ground almonds and eggs.

Pour the filling mixture into the pastry case, place the plums on top cut side up and sprinkle with an extra 2-3 tablespoons sugar. Put the tart on the hot baking tray and cook for 50-55 minutes until completely set and nicely browned.

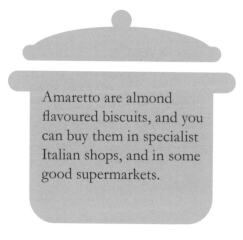

Amaretto are almond flavoured biscuits, and you can buy them in specialist Italian shops, and in some good supermarkets.

THE BALLYMORE INN LEMON TART

This is the classic exam piece for pastry chefs, but you don't need lots of experience to give it a go, just watch the following. Don't over whip the filling as it will separate during the cooking into two layers, not the end of the world but not perfect. Make sure the pastry case is fully cooked, dry and sandy before you add the filling.

[12 SLICES /1 HOUR PREPARATION, PLUS 45 MINUTES BAKING /MODERATE]

28cm pastry case cooked (see page 178)

300g caster sugar
7 eggs
5 lemons, juice and rind finely grated
250ml cream, lightly whipped

icing sugar, for glazing

Set the oven to Gas 4/180˚C and place a flat baking sheet in the oven. Lightly beat the sugar and eggs together, add the lemon juice and rind. Fold in the cream and mix well. Pour the filling into the pastry case, place on the hot baking sheet, reduce the heat to Gas 2/150˚C and bake for 45 minutes or until just set. Remove from the oven, dust generously with icing sugar and glaze with a blow torch (looks good but not essential). Serve with caramel sauce (see page 192), optional.

To give the pastry case an extra seal before you add the filling, brush the inside of the pastry case with a little egg yolk and bake for another 2-3mins. then pour in the filling and bake.

CHOCOLATE CHEESECAKE

If you place the cheesecake in a cold oven, just before you turn it on, you'll find the cheesecake less likely to have a cracked top, which won't affect the delicious taste just the appearance.

[SERVES 8 /30 MINUTES PREPARATION, PLUS 70 MINUTES COOKING /EASY]

line a 26cm x 7cm spring form tin with non stick baking paper

biscuit base
250g biscuits, crushed finely
50g butter melted

450g chocolate, broken into pieces
500g mascarpone
200g golden caster sugar
1 teaspoon vanilla extract
6 eggs
2 generous tablespoons crème fraiche

Line a 26cm diameter, 7cm deep, spring-form tin with non-stick baking paper. Mix the biscuits and butter together and spread over the base of the tin.
Melt the chocolate in a large bowl on a low setting in the microwave until it's fully melted, stir well and set aside. Mix all other ingredients in the processor, fold the mixture gently into the melted chocolate and pour the lot into the prepared tin.
Place cheesecake in the oven, set the temperature to Gas 3/170°C and bake for 70 minutes until set but with a slight wobble in the centre. Turn off the oven, open the oven door slightly and allow the cheesecake to cool in the oven. Serve dusted with icing sugar.

We use our chocolate chip cookies which are delicious for the base, but you can use any shortbread or digestive type biscuit.

PASSION FRUIT and LIME CHEESECAKE

This is a delicious comfort food dessert especially during the winter months when other fruits are out of season

[SERVES 8 /30 MINUTES PREPARATION PLUS 45 MINUTES COOKING /EASY]

20cm spring form tin

biscuit base
150g shortbread biscuits (see page 161)
or use digestive biscuits
50g butter melted

filling
500g mascarpone
100ml crème fraiche
100g caster sugar
2 tablespoons cornflour
3 eggs, beaten
150ml passion fruit
  pulp
juice & rind of 1 lime

caramel
100g caster sugar
5 tablespoons water
100ml passion fruit
  pulp

When buying passion fruit choose those that feel heavy for their size with firm slightly wrinkled skins. They can be ripened further at room temperature but don't store in the fridge. To prepare slice in half and spoon out the juicy pulp. Depending on the size you'll need about 12 passion fruit for 250ml pulp.

Grease a 20cm spring-form tin with a little butter and line the base with non-stick paper. Preheat oven to Gas 4/180°C. Crush the biscuits to a fine crumb in the processor and pulse in the melted butter, spread biscuit mix evenly over the base of the tin and set aside while you make the filling.

In a large bowl, mix the mascarpone, crème fraiche and sugar together until smooth. Sift the cornflour into the mixture and stir in the beaten eggs a little at a time. Mix in the passion fruit pulp with the juice and rind of a lime. Pour the lot into the biscuit base and bake for 45 minutes, until golden; it should still have a slight wobble in the centre. Remove from the oven and cool.

To make the caramel, place the sugar in a medium pan and heat until it just turns amber colour, then carefully add the water and boil until the sugar dissolves completely. Remove from the heat, stir in the passion fruit pulp and set aside to cool. Serve the caramel with the sliced cheesecake and an optional bowl of whipped cream.

INDEX

The Ballymore Inn

We opened the doors of The Ballymore Inn, in the little village of Ballymore Eustace in County Kildare, almost twenty years ago.

We were guided by our philosophy that the best food comes from carefully selected ingredients, infused with an imaginative simplicity. The Ballymore Inn has evolved over the years but this philosophy has remained the same.

We grow our own seasonal fruit and vegetables, and we work with some of the country's best food producers and suppliers to ensure the finest dining experience for our customers.

In both the restaurant and the Back Bar we have tried to maintain the style and atmosphere of a classic country inn, thereby creating the ideal ambience for you to enjoy the dishes which we create with our dedicated staff.

Together with our fantastic team, we look forward to welcoming you to The Ballymore Inn.

The Ballymore Inn,
Main Street,
Ballymore Eustace,
County Kildare

Tel: 353 45 864585
theballymoreinn@gmail.com

www.ballymoreinn.com
https://www.facebook.com/BallymoreInn